Essays on the Crisis
in Lebanon

GW00602775

Edited by Roger Owen

CONTENTS

Ithaca Press London

First published in 1976 by
Ithaca Press   13 Southwark Street   London   SE1
Printed in England by
Anchor Press Ltd   and bound by Brendon and Sons Ltd
both of Tiptree   Essex
ISBN 0 903729 18 0

INTRODUCTION

The essays contained herein were originally presented as papers to a small seminar held at the Middle East Centre of St Antony's College in December 1975. Our aim was, jointly, to arrive at a better understanding of the Lebanese crisis by looking at aspects of the political and economic development of the country both in the past and immediate present. In revising these papers for publication each author has presented a very personal interpretation of events. But if there is a common theme it is the need to understand the crisis in terms of the progressive breakdown of a specifically Lebanese system of government and society in which the economic structure, political institutions and communal leadership were all interlocked in such a way as to resist change and to be unable to accommodate new forces. In 1958 a civil war in which an estimated 2,500 people were killed produced only the mild reforms of President Chehab's Presidency. By December 1975 another 7,000 or so people had been killed in a second war for what then seemed to be the introduction of a neo-Chehabist programme sponsored by the Syrians and some elements on the Lebanese Right and Left. It is towards an understanding of this system, of its resistance to change, of the conflict which threatened its breakdown and of the rival attempts to put it together again that these essays are directed.

Roger Owen

THE CREATION OF THE LEBANESE ECONOMY - ECONOMIC GROWTH IN THE NINETEENTH AND TWENTIETH CENTURIES

by Paul Saba

The development of the Lebanese economy in the nineteenth and early twentieth centuries was a process involving two contrary, opposing dynamics. In the middle decades of the nineteenth century the feudal economy began to crumble under the impact of a rapid expansion of the European trade and of Lebanese merchant and usurious capital. What characterized the subsequent history of this economy, however, was the way in which the same set of forces, having dislocated the found- ations of the feudal order and encouraged the emergence of capitalist relations, limited the scope of these relations or stunted and retarded their fuller development. The first of these dynamics was the underlying impetus to the political upheavals of the mid eighteen-hundreds; the second influenced the broad course of this economy's development from that date until well into the present century.

The most far reaching and disruptive consequence of the movement of trade and usury in the middle decades of the nineteenth century was the destruction of the political and economic power of the feudal ruling class. The basic revenue of this class consisted of a regular portion of the land tax collected on behalf of the Ottoman Government, as well as of a rent taken in kind from peasant cultivators, who worked either as landless serfs or metayers, or combined their primary labour as metayers with the cultivation of their own small parcels. The amount of this rent was determined in accordance with the nature of the product and on the basis of customary, written or oral contracts. The portion of the product taken as basic tax and rent, moreover, was often augmented by additional portions exacted as irregular or special taxes or surtaxes, as well as by a regular series of gifts and dues demanded of peasants on a number of holidays, religious feast days, and other occasions.

The portion of the total product appropriated in these ways by the ruling landowners - a small number of titled families of chaykhs and emirs - has been estimated at up to 75 percent. But the portion of the product accruing to these families in the form of money was considerably smaller. Nearly all peasant villages engaged in a variety of productions - wheat and other grains, vegetables, fruits, cheese, tobacco, wine, olive oil, wool, raw cotton and raw silk - the whole or major portions of which were directly consumed by the peasants themselves and the chaykhs or emirs for whom they laboured. It was only the surplus of any of these products which was available for exchange, a process which took place in small local markets organized on fixed dates, and which was effected primarily by barter. In the sixteenth, seventeenth and eighteenth centuries, nevertheless, certain quantities of some of these products were also involved in a wider system of exchange and constituted the principal sources of money revenue in various areas of Lebanese territory Such was the case with portions of the tobacco, cotton and wood produced in the districts south of Saida and of the olive oil and raw silk produced in the region north of this port, which were purchased partly by European merchants, and partly by merchant caravans arrived from Egypt or from the interior Syrian cities of Damascus, Homs, Hama, and Aleppo. Taken in its entirety, however, the Lebanese economy in these centuries was characrerized by a limited volume of marketable production and by the widespread prevalence of barter exchange.

The movement which led to the undermining of feudal rule began with a series of gradual developments, within this limited structure of production and exchange, which date from the end of the eighteenth century. In the traditional grain growing region of the Beqaa there was an extension of the cultivation of wheat, while in certain westerly districts of the Lebanon mountain range there was a growth of cultivation of the mulberry tree, the principal source of nourishment of the silk worm. In the middle of the last decade of the eighteenth century an important trade in grain began to develop in the village of

Zahle, which was favoured for this activity by its location on the eastern slope of the Lebanese mountains on the approaches to the Beqaa.
From about the same period there also began to develop, in Zahle itself,
Dayr al-Qamar, Zouk Mikayil, and a number of other villages in the
district of Bikfaya, a growth of handicraft production, in particular
of silk and cotton cloth, for a market far wider than the immediate
vicinity or environs in which these villages were located. The impetus
for the trade in grain may have come, in the first instance, from an
increased European demand occasioned by the French Revolution and
the Napoleonic wars; it was furthered by the expropriation, on the part
of the Ottoman Governor of Saida, of the grain and other crops in one
of the westerly districts of the Lebanon mountain range, as well as by
the gradual extension of mulberry growing, which was likely to have
taken place at the expense of the cultivation of wheat. The impetus for
the development of mulberry cultivation, on the other hand, was evidently
linked to a growing demand for raw silk on the Egyptian market as a
result of the agrucultural and industrial policies of Muhammed Ali Pacha,
and possibly to an increased demand by the weaving industry of the
interior Syrian cities, in the wake of the falling off of European imports
of cloth. These latter developments may in turn have influenced the
growth of the handicraft weaving industry, many of whose silk and
cotton articles came to be marketed during this period not only in various parts of Lebanese territory, but also in the interior cities of Syria
and in parts of Palestine, as well as in Anatolia, Salonica, and Egypt.

The gradual effects of these developments were a spread and
penetration of money transactions in various areas of the barter economy, an enlarging of the scope for small accumulations among peasant
and artisan producers, and a growing involvement of these or of other
individuals in the slowly widening sphere of trade and exchange. There
is evidence during this period for the growth in importance of small
village mills as a source of money income, a develpment which may
have been favoured by the replacing of wheat by mulberry growing. Many
of these mills were owned by feudal rulers themselves or by monasteries,
but a number of them were built and owned, evidently with the permission
of chaykhs and emirs, either by peasant families or by individuals who
acted as supervisors or intendants of feudal properties. In the first half
of the nineteenth century, some of these mills were apparently employed
in a gradual, growing commercial production of flour.

Other developments favoured accumulations by peasants engaged in
the cultivation of the mulberry tree and the production of silk-worm

cocoons. The increased cultivation of the mulberry tree was often encouraged - especially in districts with a relative scarcity of population -
by the use of a contract for metayage which gave to cultivators the ownership of half of a newly planted parcel of land after a lapse of a fixed
number of years. From the early years of the nineteenth century there
were peasants who, having acquired land in this way, were able to obtain
extra money income from the increased volume of their disposable
surplus. The growth of mulberry cultivation and of the production of
silk worm cocoons also gave to other peasants - with skills in the evaluation
of mulberry yields or in certain processes of silk-worm rearing -
additional opportunities for work which they could be compensated in
money or in a product for which the demand was growing.

There were corresponding opportunities in artisan spheres. Although
fuller information is lacking, there is evidence for the existence during
this period of small weaving workshops in certain of the artisan villages,
some of which employed hired labourers and may have been owned by
peasant - handicraftsmen who, aided by members of their family, had
accumulated surplus sums as a result of the widening of the market for
silk and cotton cloth. Opportunities for small accumulations were also
available to other producers. In the second decade of the nineteenth century,
silk thread spinners from the Lebanese mountains were able to find extra work outside of their districts by descending to the coastal plains
surrounding Beirut. There is a revealing example of this period of
a handicraftsman named Hayik, in the northerly village of Bichmizzin,
who arrived at this village in the early years of the nineteenth century
and earned his livelihood by spinning into thread silk-worm cocoons
produced by peasants who either did not own a spinning wheel or for
some other reason could not accomplish this task- in time this handicraftsman accumulated enough money to begin buying up silk thread
from other producers and marketing it in Beirut.

This putting to use of free money in the sphere of trade was an
important aspect of the movement within the Lebanese economy in the
early decades of the nineteenth century. However, surplus sums were
obtained - whether through productive agricultural or artisan labour, or
in return for the performance of regular services for chaykhs and emirs,
such as the supervision of their properties, the collection of taxes at village
level, or by secretarial and accounting activities - the general conditions
of development in these decades encouraged the transformation of such
sums into trading capital. The family Khairallah, of the village of Jrane
in the district of Batround, were favoured during this period by the Emir

Bachir Chehab with a grant of land in full ownership; in time this family of peasant producers, aided by the cultivation of additional land, was
able to accumulate enough money for one of its sons to give up agricultural
labour and begin to trade in silk. The head of the family Michaqqa, of
the village of Dayr al-Qamar, was a salaried secretary to the Emir
Bachir Chehab, while his sons were all accomplished artisans. At the
end of the second decade of the nineteenth century, this family began to
combine its secretarial and handicraft occupations with trade. A similar
course was evidently followed by another inhabitant of Dayr al-Qamar
named Butrus Jawich, who was employed by the Emir Bachir Chehab as
a treasurer and accountant at a salary of 4500 piastres per year; in
1882 this individual was also regarded as "one of the most considerable
silk merchants" of this village.

In the first four or five decades of the nineteenth century, as noted
above, the weaving industry of Lebanon developed to the point where its
silk and cotton articles were widely marketed throughout the Ottoman
Empire. Although little specific information exists on the economic
relations which developed in this industry, it is more likely that its
gradual growth gave rise, from among the cloth producers themselves, to
a certain number of buyers-up - individuals who circulated among the
artisan craftsmen, brought up their production, and arranged for its marketing in Beirut and elsewhere. There is evidence from as early as 1810
about the important activities of buyers-up, from Zahlr, Dayr al-Qamar,
and other villages, in purchasing sheep from the Arab and Kurdish tribes-
men who pastured their flocks in the highlands of the district of Jbyal.
The opportunities created for trading capital during these decades were
evidently not lost on the small, established merchant communities of the
coastal towns. In 1821, under the pressure of political circumstances,
it was reported that the 'substantial merchants of the port of Akka,
left this town, some of them for Beirut, and some for Lebanon.'

The increased of regional specialization in agriculture, the development of handicraft production for a wider market, the growth of certain
villages into centres of trade and artisan activity, and the gradual,
widening development of money wealth independent of that of the ruling
chaykhs and emirs - the whole of this movement was clearly observable
from the early years of the nineteenth century. At the same time, however,
this movement remained tightly confined within the boundaries of feudal
control. The relationship of the mass of peasant producers to their
ruling landowners continued to be characterized by a high degree of
personal dependence and direct physical servitude. There were peasants

who could not marry without the permission of the chaykh or emir for whom they laboured; others who could not receive visitors or offer them hospitality outside the residence of their feudal ruler. Although certain contracts of metayage indicated that peasants were at liberty to terminate a contract and to work for another landowner, in practice this liberty could be realized only with the permission of the chaykh or emir concerned or by actual physical flight.

In addition to these ties of personal dependence, peasant-artisan producers were also often subjected to a variety of forced labour services. There were peasants who, in addition to cultivating their ordinary rented parcels, were also made to work a certain number of days on other, specially designated parcels, the whole product of which was reserved by chaykhs and emirs for their expenses of hospitality and entertainment. The Egyptian administration, through the intermediary of Lebanese feudal rulers, made use of forced peasant labour for work in the coal and iron mines of the Lebanese mountains. The chronicler Haydar Chehab speaks at an earlier date of the construction of a canal on behalf of the Emir Bachie, which was accomplished over the course of three years by the uncompensated labour of the villagers living along its route, and also of the construction of a bridge, on the northerly river of Nahr al Kebir, the expenses for which were sharply reduced, because only the "master artisans were compensated, while the labourers worked without pay." Labour services were also imposed on the women of peasant families. There are examples of peasant women or girls who were made to set aside their own domestic or agricultural labours and forced to perform various tasks in the residences or households of their ruling chaykhs.

Nor was the development of independent money wealth able to proceed without regular harassments or sharp interventions by chaykhs and emirs. Gifts and dues, some of which required money outlays (soap, sugar, coffee), continued to be demanded of peasants on a wide and regular variety of occasions. There is evidence from the 1840s and 1850s that mules and muleteers, some of them apparently employed by merchants, were sometimes commandeered by the ruling authorities and subjected to forced labour services. Chaykhs and emirs tried, moreover, through new taxes and forced exactions, to appropriate for themselves as much as possible of the wealth created by the gradual development of production and trade. With the growth of the weaving industry in Dayr al-Qamar, the looms of this village were subjected to a tax of 30 piastres per year, and in the early 1830s village grain mills also became the object of a special tax. For the purposes of taxation, the Khazen

chaykhs attempted to control the trade in silk in the district of Kesruwan by routing it all through the village of Zouk Mikayil. The Abillama
emirs took advantage of the developing trade of Zahle to impose a tax on the
purchase and sale of grain. According to the Lebanese author of a
history of Zahle, the Emir Bachir Chehab regularly 'borrowed' from the
inhabitants of this town sums ranging between 40,000 and 100,000 piastres, without reimbursing them. Another author claims that the same
Emir used to boast of Dayr al-Qamar: "its merchants were for money
in time of need, its men were for warfare."

The bonds of feudal control were broken in the middle decades of
the nineteenth century in the course of a swift and widespread expansion
of merchant and usurious capital. This expansion was generated in
the flow of a rapidly developing trade with Europe, in particular with
Britain and France. Between 1827 and 1862 the amount of trade passing
through Beirut, measured in francs, increased ninefold. During the
same period, the population of this town grew from 6,000 - 8,000 to
perhaps 40, - 50,000. The principal impetus for this growth was the
establishment of foreign consulates and of both foreign and Lebanese
merchant and moneydealing houses.

The effects of this development were ramified throughout the feudal
economy. Beirut merchant houses not only engaged in purchases and
sales through individuals commissioned directly by them; they also
forwarded money and merchandise to the smaller, peasant - artisan
traders, or to feudal attendants who had taken up trade, in villages throughout
the Lebanese interior. The development of this network of links was
reflected in the steady growth of certain of these villages in the course
of the middle decades of the century. Between 1825 and 1860, the population of Zahle rose from 4,000 - 5,000 to 10,000. The population of
Dayr al-Qamar, in a somewhat longer span of time, increased from
4,000 to 12 - 15,000. The village of Hasbaya, which at the beginning of
the nineteenth century was a small agglomeration not far from a regular
stop on the east - west caravan route, by 1860 was a trading centre
with 200 shops and a population of more than 6,000. The establishment
of this network of links contrasted sharply with the procedures of exchange
in the sixteenth, seventeenth and eighteenth centuries and corresponded
directly to a liaison between European and Lebanese trading interests.
What was even more striking, however, was the extent to which the
money and merchandise flowing in this network were transformed into
usurious capital.

The immediate circumstances for this transformation were a rise

of basic money expenses and concurrent decline of money income.
Money expenses increased acutely during the period of the Egyptian
occupation, which lasted from 1832 to 1840.   The consumption of the
occupying army drove up the prices of sheep and wheat - the two
indispensible purchases made by the inhabitants of the Lebanon mountain range - while the tax burden imposed by the Egyptian administration, according to the most conservative estimates, increased by at
least two and one-half times.   Nor were chaykhs and emirs able to take
advantage of this increase in their capacity as tax collectors.   Not only
did the Egyptian administration raise the level of taxes generally, it
also deprived the Lebanese feudal rulers of their right to retain an arbitrary portion of these taxes, and substituted for this portion a fixed payment 'which did not exceed a tenth of what they used to collect.'
    Despite the Egyptian withdrawal in 1840, the pressure created by
taxes continued to be felt throughout the next decade.   The principal
reason for this was the application of the Tariff Treaty of 1838, con-
cluded in that year between the Ottoman Government and the government
of Britain and France.   The effect of this treaty was to encourage
merchants and traders in the Lebanese districts of Ottoman territory
to deduct from the price of products purchased for export the percentage
of the new, higher duty imposed on them, and to surcharge in the same
way the price of wheat or other basic purchases.   The   chronicle   of
Tannous al Chidyaq, which seldom deals with financial or economic
matters, offers evidence that the new customs arrangements went some
way toward negating the reduction of the land and capitation tax which
was promised to Lebanese feudal rulers in the wake of the Egyptian
withdrawal.   According to this account, the chaykhs and emirs sharply complained of the incidence of the new tariffs, but were told that
'were it not for the customs, the /other taxes/ would be higher.'
    Expenses created by the tax burden were increased by a number
of other circumstances.   Speaking of the Lebanese ruling families in
the middle decades of the nineteenth century, a Lebanese contemporary
wrote that the growth in size of these families, which increased their
basic living expenses, was a principal cause of their decline. Whether
the luxury expenses of these families were also increased by the attraction of a widening variety of European imports it is impossible to
say;   there are striking examples, on the other hand, of other kinds
of wasteful expenditures - huge sums for political bribes, the expenses
of equipping and supplying armed partisans - which were made by
individual chaykhs and emirs and drove them deeply into debt.   Other ·

expenses were more generally incurred by the widening pattern of the foreign trade itself. By 1860, the growing European purchases of skins, hides and woold had driven up the price of sheep; the same may also have been true of wheat, especially during the period of increased demand created by the Crimean War.

What aggravated the pressure created by these expenses was a steady decline of money income. One of the major consequences of the expanded European trade was to shrink the internal market for the raw silk and cotton produced by Lebanese peasants. As early as 1831, the 1000 looms of Zahle virtually stopped producing cottons under the pressure of competition from British-made cloth. In the early 1830s, more than 25,000 weaving looms, producing a half silk and half cotton cloth, were operating in Damascus and Aleppo; although individual estimates vary, the weight of evidence suggests that by the early 1850s, the number of these looms had declined by at leastt one half and possibly more. At about the same time, perhaps as few as 40 looms - down from 300 - were operating in the village of Zouk Mikayil, while the several hundred looms of Dayr al-Qamar were being put out of use by the activities of some twenty five merchants in this town engaged in the marketing of imported cloth. Probably beginning in this same decade, the artisan looms of the district of Bikfaya ceased altogether to produce silk cloth and survived only by the production of a specially cotton item known as the 'Dima'. The raw cotton and dyes necessary for this production, however, were no longer obtained in Syria and Lebanon but were purchased from importers in Beirut. Although import-export and price movements cannot be examined in detail here, the effect of the import of European cloth was to reduce substantially the income derived from two of the principle sources of money revenue in the feudal economy. In the case of peasant - produced raw silk this decline was perhaps less sharp since a growing proportion of this item, unlike cotton, was purchased during this period for the export market; but it was significant nevertheless, insofar as prices on this market were unfavourable.

It was this conjecture of circumstances - the increase of expenses, the decline of revenue, and the growing influx of European money and manufactures - which formed the dynamic for the expansion of usury. Of the twenty wealthiest individuals of Dayr al-Qamar from the beginning of the second half of the nineteenth century, at least five were active primarily as moneylenders. Small traders during this period were prepared to sell their European manufacturers at a loss in order to obtain sums which could be put to more profitable use in moneylending; or else they borrowed money from Beirut merchant houses at six per cent interest and liquidated this debt by charging their own debtors twenty per cent, thirty per cent, or more. In the middle decades of the nineteenth century, the sons and grandsons of the Emir Bachir Chehab were in debt to the Beirut trading house of Matar; Chaykh Qansuh al-Khazen was in debt to the merchant families Lahoud and Tabit; Chaykh Said Jumblat was in debt to a merchant of 'modest origin' named Habib Doumani; the Emir Ahmad Abillama was in debt to the Beirut merchant house of Toubiya and Asfar; the Emir Amin Arslan was in debt to the merchant brothers Ibrahim and Rustum Baz, as were the emirs Munqith and Salim Chehab. In 1850 the Emir Bachir Chehab died apparently owing money to the brothers Khalil and Milhem Traboulsi, merchants from Dayr al-Qamar. In 1860 the Emir Ahmad Abillama died in debt to Elyas al-Munnayir, a merchant from the village of Zouk Mikayil. At the time of his death in 1861, the accumulated debts of Chaykh Said Jumblat had reached 1,000,000 piastres. Speaking of the feudal ruling families in the middle of the nineteenth century, a Lebanese merchant contemporary estimated that the sum of their debts, with interest, amounted to fifty per cent of their revenues. The same author also described the ruin and impoverishment of the mass of peasant and artisan producers: thousands fled to Beirut and other cities of Syria and Egypt and reduced to begging; thousands more labouring for day wages as haulers of stone, earth and clay in building works; others surviving as menial servants in the shops or households of the urban rich.

These troubled middle decades of the nineteenth century are the period most studied in the modern history of Lebanon. They were marked by three major outbursts of fighting and bloodshed between Christians and Druzes, in 1841, 1845, and 1860, as well as by a destructive, prolonged peasant revolt in the northerly district of Kesruwan, in 1858-59. Many accepted accounts or studies of this period have emphasized the emergence of sectarian feeling as its most important and distinguishing characteristic, but in doing so, they have implied that the revolt of 1858-59, which was an upsurge of Christian peasants against the Christian chaykhs Khazen, was a distinct event bearing little relation to the sectarian clashes of the central and southerly districts. In fact all of these major eruptions of violence, together with the growth of sectarian consciousness, can be more fully and consistently explained if they are viewed against the background of the economic movement which was shattering the stability of the feudal order.

As feudal rulers fell more deeply into debt and ceded or sold parcels of their land, they tried to diminish their growing losses by increased taxes and forced exactions. The pressure created by their deepening indebtment and the harsher exploitation which it provoked, was released in a bitter political struggle over control of land, the power of taxation, and the rights and privileges of the ruling families. A widespread growth of metayage was reported in the middle decades of the nineteenth century, as individual peasant cultivators, who possessed or had acquired parcels of land in full ownership in addition to those which they rented from chaykhs, lost these parcels forcibly to feudal rulers and were reduced to working them as metayers. A French consul reported in 1844 a large number of disputes over ownership of land in the central-southerly districts of the Lebanon mountain range, and the political settlement of the following year, arranged by the Ottoman Government, aimed at regulating the distribution of the land tax and at protecting villagers against arbitrary exactions; in practice, however, its provisions were ignored by the ruling chaykhs and emirs. In the bloody series of violent clashes which preceded this settlement, many titles to landed property, acquired by individual village families, were destroyed or looted by chaykhs and their armed retainers, while the cadastral survey authorized by the Ottomon Government in the latter part of this decade was abandoned in 1849 as a result of harassment by feudal rulers.

Events at the end of the following decade were a violent continuation of this struggle. In 1858 and 1859, peasants in the northerly district of Kesruwan rose up against the chaykhs of the family Khazen, demanding an equalized distribution of the land tax, the abolition of the right to authorize marriages, an end to the exaction of gifts and dues and the imposition of forced labour services, and an abolition of contrived taxes on land sold by chaykhs to villagers. In 1859 there were lesser peasant disturbances in parts of the central-southerly districts as well, and in the following year, massacres were carried out by Druze chaykhs and their partisans in several parts of these districts, much of the most intense fighting or greatest loss of life occurring in the towns of Zahle and Dayr al-Qamar and the important trading centre of Hasbaya.

The flaring of intense sectarian feeling was an important development within these decades, but studies which account for this development in terms of the policies of the Egyptian administration and of the deposed Emir Bachir Chehab, the rivalries of British and French imperialisms, the growing ambitiousness of the Maronite Patriarch, and the desire of the Ottoman Government to regain and strengthen control of its Lebanese districts, provide only a partial explanation – one which places too little emphasis on the economic movement which was rupturing feudal property relations and the self-perceptions which corresponded to them.

In the sixteenth, seventeenth, and eighteenth centuries, as in the middle of the nineteenth, individuals in the Lebanese social order also possessed a strong sense of themselves as followers of a specific religion or rite, but this sense was part of a fuller self-consciousness involving equally important identities as metayers, dependents, and adherents of individual chaykhs and emirs. In the middle of the nineteenth century, when the expansion of usury and trade began to break up the properties of the ruling families, these latter identities became less secure. Peasants were in one season giving up their product to the chaykh or emir for whom they had always laboured and to whom they were attached, and in the next turning it over to the new landowners to whom these rulers had been forced to cede or sell their property. When, in the so-called 'mixed districts,' chaykhs tried to recoup their losses by surtaxing the product appropriated by these owners, or by intensifying their exploitation of peasants themselves, the disruption of established property relations quickened susceptibilities to sectarian appeals. Challenged and indebted Druze chaykhs, a growing number of Christian merchants, usurers, buyers-up, and better-to-do peasant landowners, and the mass of Druze and Christian peasants - all were caught up in a bitter struggle in which attempts to arouse sectarian identity - on the part of Druze chaykhs, in their Druze peasants, on the part of Christian landowners, in Christian metayers - could be used to resist the rupture of feudal authority, or to advance new claims to property and political rights. A study of the property holdings of the Maronite Church, moreover, which it has not been possible to accomplish until now, would be likely to provide a fuller explanation for the growing political assertiveness of the Maronite Patriarch during this period, who in 1841, was urging on Christians in the districts of the Chouf and the Maten against the ruling Druze chaykhs, and in 1858 tended to support, although more reservedly, the peasants of Kesruwan against the Christian chaykhs of the family Khazen. A certain amount of Church property was exempt from taxation, and in a period of growing economic pressure, it is conceivable that indebted chaykhs and emirs, both Christian and Druze, turned to this property as a source of additional revenue.

In broad terms the whole of the upheaval in the middle decades of the nineteenth century must be regarded in the first instance as a political and economic struggle involving, on the one side, the feudal ruling class, and on the other, the mass of oppressed and exploited peasants, the Maronite Church and its dependencies, and an emerging class of merchants, moneylenders, and better-to-do villagers and peasant landowners.

Whatever the precise effect of this struggle on the growth of sectarian feeling, its political outcome was the defeat of the feudal ruling class. The political settlement which emerged in the early 1860s, arranged by the Ottoman Government under the pressure of European force of arms, declared an end to all privileges of the ruling families and made the collection of taxes a function of salaried officials under the direct authority of an Ottoman Governor.   The distribution of taxes, by district and village, was determined by an administrative council sitting at the side of this Governor, whose twelve members were elected by district assemblies of village chaykhs, themselves chosen by property holders in elections within each village.   With the loss of their power of arbitrary taxation, the last, tenuous hold of chaykhs and emirs on their landed property was broken, and the alienation of this property proceeded more rapidly.   In 1862 an order was issued by the Ottoman Governor for the registration, in newly established courts, of all sales of immovable property, and in the middle years of the 1860s, a cadastral survey was finally carried out and completed.   Although adequate figures have never existed on the extent of land owned by the ruling families, it has been estimated that by the end of the nineteenth century, the portion of the national wealth retained by these families had declined from perhaps 75 per cent to between 25 per cent and 10 per cent.

With respect to the development of the Lebanese economy, this rapid expansion of the trade with Europe, and of Lebanese merchant and usurious capital, was a dynamic impetus to the emergence of capitalist relations, in various spheres and areas of production, throughout the latter half of the nineteenth century.   Probably beginning in the 1840s or 1850s, capitalist relations developed in the course of the disruption of the domestic weaving industry in the district of Bikfaya, as independent peasant-artisan producers became wage workers in a fairly extended 'putting-out' system.   In the 1840s and 1850s, thirty silk-reeling manufactories, employing an average of 70-80 hired workers, were established under similar circumstances: their owners were attracted to this investment by the prospect of paying cheap wages to ruined silk spinners or silk cloth weavers or to young women or girls from indebted peasant families, as well as by the prospect of obtaining silk cocoons at prices cheapened by usurious advances.   The free operation of these manufactures, however, was in many cases hindered by individual feudal rulers, who, themselves indebted to manufactory owners or challenged by them in their traditional authority over village families, asserted themselves against the interests of these owners with respect to the recovery of their debts or the recruitment and hiring of peasant workers.

The establishment of certain democratic rights as the outcome of
the struggle of these decades widened the scope for capitalist developments.   For a large segment of Lebanese peasants, the abolition of
feudal dues and privileges, together with the continuing break up of the
ruling families' property, at least dissolved the most onerous ties bind-
ing them to their landlords.   To the merchants and usurers whose land
they came to cultivate, or to the buyers up to whom they sold the product
of their own small parcels, peasants were often deeply in debt and subject to harsh economic dependence, but the full disposition of their own
labour time, as well as that of their wives and daughters, and their right
to obtain other work in addition to their ordinary tasks of cultivation, were
no longer obstructed by the personal dependence and physical coercion
which characterized their relations with chaykhs and emirs.   The stabili-
sation of the tax system, moreover, and the emergence of democratic
forms of administration, however limited, provided the general political
conditions in which money wealth could finally be accumulated without
harassments by feudal rulers or the threat of direct expropriation by
them;   they thereby gave an important impetus to that process of differentiation among peasant families which had been developing from the
early decades of the century but was retarded by the interventions of
chaykhs and emirs.   From the early years of the 1860s, the redistribu-
tion to peasant cultivators of certain feudal properties;   the acquisition
of other properties by the extension of mulberry cultivation on the basis
of the contract for metayage referred to above, or with money obtained
from high cocoon prices in the 1860s and 1870s;   the corresponding, continuing expansion of a market for wheat in the Lebanon mountain range;
the development or resumption of a demand for a number of other agricultural or processed agricultural products (olive oil, tobacco, and
grapes);   the gradual emergence of a regular summer resort season,
which created opportunities for the marketing of surplus fruits and vegetables or the rental of individual village properties - all of these developments, together with the destruction of feudal political rule, gave impetus
to the gradual, continuing emergence of a grouping of richer peasant
families, who were encouraged to take advantage of their acquisitions of
land and of the freer conditions for obtaining a work force by investing in
capitalist productive activities.

Examples of such activities increase throughout the latter decades
of the century.   Several sources attest to the use of hired labourers in
agriculture as early as the 1830s and 1840s, and this practice evolved
slowly in the following decades.   Both seasonal and day wage-workers,

many of them migrating from the Lebanese mountains, were employed
in the olive groves of the district of Chwayfat, in parts of the wheat growing region of the Beqaa, in mulberry plantations in the coastal district
between Beirut and Damour, and in the forests of the districts of Akkar
and Hermel, where peasants from villages in the Maten, for example,
migrated each summer and worked in the extraction of resin and tar.

There were corresponding developments in manufacturing spheres.
In the 1860s and 1870s, some 200 individuals living in the vicinity of Dayr
al-Qamar, made their way to this town each day where they were employed in small workshops - several of which had eight or more hired workers -
in a cobbling and shoe-making industry. With the ending in practice of
forced labour services, road building and other construction works often
came to be undertaken from this period by individual contractors employing hired artisans and other workmen; there are examples of formal
agreements between such contractors and the administrative council of
Mount Lebanon. In the last two or three decades of the nineteenth century, a certain number of handicraft tanning and leather-working shops
in Zahle were owned by rich merchants of this town, and the same was
probably also true of a number of the 40 or 50 workshops involved in the
production of wine and araq. During the same period, perhaps 10-20
grain and olive oil mills, using modern equipment, were set up both in
Beirut and in various villages of the Lebanese mountains; the oil-making
enterprises employed an average of up to twelve hired workers. In the
middle of the 1880s, at least fourteen soap works, each employing perhaps
ten workers, were observed to be operating at various locations in
Lebanese territory; although insofar as some of these works were located in the Lebanese mountains, their establishment appears to have
occurred only from the middle decades of the century, since the fabrication of soap until that time was a monopoly confined to artisans of Dayr-
al-Qamar. In the first decade of the 1900s a small lace-making industry
developed along capitalist lines, as Lebanese merchants, acting as agents
for French and American trading houses, began to furnish needles, thread
and patterns to peasant women for the fabrication of lace articles in their
households against the payment of piece-wages. In 1888 a paper manufactory, employing 100 workers, was established with Lebanese capital
in the coastal village of Antelias. In the last decade of the nineteenth
century and the early years of the 1900s, 200 small tobacco-curing and
cigarette-making workshops, each employing perhaps 10-20 male and
female workers, were established in many villages in the tobacco-growing
districts of the Lebanon mountain range. An even more considerable
development occurred in the case of the silk industry, where as many as

200 village reeling manufactories, averaging more than 50 wage-workers, were set up in the latter decades of the century in addition to the 30 earlier manufactories established in the 1840s and 1850s.

What charact erized the dynamic of the Lebanese economy from the middle decades of the nineteenth century, however, was the way in which capitalist relations, once having emerged, were retarded or limited in their fuller development under the impact of the same basic forces which had quickened the conditions for their coming into being. Three brief examples will illustrate this process more clearly.

With the growth of the weaving industry in the villages of the district of Bikfaya capitalist relations may have begun to emerge as early as the first half of the nineteenth century, as differentiation developed among artisan producers or as individual merchants or buyers up either invested in small, weaving workshops, or began giving out raw materials for their fabrication in peasant households. It is clear, nevertheless, that the vast majority of producers in this industry were not hired workers but peasant-artisans who, aided by other members of their family, undertook weaving as a subsidiary of their primary agricultural labours. In the middle decades of the nineteenth century, however, while much of this basically independent domestic industry was disrupted or abandoned, the most important section which did survive came to be organized on capitalist lines. Here, the weaving, dying, and finishing of cloth were undertaken by artisans who, no longer producing at their own expense, had become daily wage or piece wage workers. There were 4200 individuals producing in this way, in the employment of some thirty 'owners,' who were in turn dependent on Beirut merchants, from whom they obtained raw cotton and dyes, and to whom they sold their finished articles.

To what extent these merchants themselves had taken the initiative in organizing this industry it is difficult to say; what appears clear, however, is that throughout the latter half of the nineteenth century, neither they nor the thirty owner-employers either advanced its technical foundation or its basic scale and physical organization. Production continued to take place in small village workshops or peasant households, with primitive hand looms and other basic instruments owned by the producing artisans themselves. The continuing influx of European cloth – estimated at eight times the value of that produced for export in Syria and Lebanon combined – kept up the pressure on this industry and made substantial investments in new looms or workshops, or in organization on a larger scale, a risk unequal to the promise of its return. The industry survived by the production of a single specialty cotton item known as the 'Dima,' which was circulated in the interstices of the Ottoman market.

The tobacco curing and cigarette making industry provides another
example of this process.   In the middle or latter half of the 1880s, the
introduction of a new strain of tobacco stimulated the resumption and extension of this cultivation in many of the traditional tobacco growing
districts of the Lebanese mountains.   This movement in turn eventually
gave rise, as noted above, to the establishment of some 200 small, village workshops, employing perhaps 2,000 – 4,000 hired workers from
peasant families, for the curing of tobacco and the fabrication of cigarettes.   The growth of this industry, however, also coincided with the
extension of operations of the Régie de Tabac, a company of French
shareholders which was formed in 1883 as one of the series of arrangements made by the Ottoman Government with its European creditors in
the wake of its bankruptcy in the middle of the previous decade.

By 1904 this company possessed the right to determine the localities and the conditions in which tobacco could be cultivated in the Ottoman
Empire;   the right to collect for its own account the customary tithes on
the tobacco crop;   the monopoly right to purchase the whole of the untaxed
portion of this crop;   the right to collect the customs duties on the import
and export of all tobacco products;   and the right to collect another duty
on the tobacco known as Tanbac, the sale of which by peasant cultivators
was free within Ottoman territory.   It also owned two large cigarette
and cigar manufactories in the Syrian districts of this territory, the products of which were sold for its account through the agency of local
merchants.   Not content with the revenues from these concessions and
interests, however, this company also insisted upon restricting the
market for the tobacco and cigarettes produced in the administrative district of the Lebanese mountains, where, in accordance with the political
settlement of the early 1860s, the more lately established Régie did not
obtain direct control over the production and sale of tobacco.   To this
end it demanded and obtained from the Ottoman Government measures to
prevent the smuggling of tobacco products from these mountains to the
districts lying under the direct control of the Régie, in particular to the
city of Beirut, which by the early 1900s formed a market of over 100,000
inhabitants;   and in 1912 it offered to the Ottoman authorities to make
available for the administrative budget of Mount Lebanon, in return for
tightening the measures against smuggling, 10 per cent of the revenues
obtained from the sale of tobacco products imported by it, the Régie,
into this district.   Despite the resistance of certain parties in the tobacco growing villages, this use of political pressure and of a continuing,
physical blockade, together with the influx of competing tobacco products

in the interests of the Régie and of local importers, combined to depress this industry heavily: in the years preceding the first World War, the number of village tobacco workshops declined from 200 to nor more than 80.

The third example from this period is the case of the Lebanese silk industry.   To the steady increase in the number of reeling manufactories in the latter half of the nineteenth century there corresponded an equally important growth of mulberry cultivation;   by the early 1900s perhaps 60 per cent of the cultivated area of the Lebanon mountain range was given over to the mulberry tree, with additional areas planted in the coastal plains around Beirut, Tripoli and Saida, and in the Beqaa valley and the northerly district of Akkar.   By the same period the weight of this industry in the economy of the Lebanese-Syrian districts of the Ottoman Empire was unmatched by any other: 65 per cent of the estimated value of all production in the Lebanese mountains, and 45 per cent of the total value of exports from Syria and Lebanon combined, were represented in the form of cocoons, raw silk, and silk waste.   What underlay this considerable movement in the absolute volume of production, however, was a fundamental backwardness of technique and organization which, in both the agricultural and manufacturing sphere of this industry, persisted unchanged throughout the whole period of its growth.   In the middle of the first decade of the nineteenth century, under the pressure of competition on the French market from Japanese and Chinese raw silk, this industry began its descent into full decline, to be revived briefly in the 1920s, but finally extinguished in the world depression. Its failure to modernize and sustain itself not only furnishes another illustration of the way in which the Ottoman Empire was reduced to a semi-colony of European capital in the latter half of the nineteenth century; it also provides perhaps the most revealing example of the forces at work to retard capitalist development in the Lebanese economy of this period.

The largest of the reeling manufactories were established between about 1850 and the middle of the 1880s, a number of them by Lebanese merchants (Sirsuq, Tueni, Asfar, Medawar, Freij and others) who had profited from the expansion of trade in the middle decades of the century. The new manufactories were supplied, however, by a small-scale agriculture which was primitive in technique and organization and which was ravaged for part of this period by silk worm disease;   they were producing, moreover, almost entirely for the French market.   Much of the material impetus for their establishment came from Marseille and Lyon import-export houses, which advanced to the owners of the manufactories, either directly or through intermediaries in Beirut, the

capital necessary for the large-scale purchase of cocoons and other
basic materials. These arrangements, together with the continuing influx of European cloth into the shrunken internal market, tied the manufactories to the export trade and the fluctuations of world market prices.
The fluctuations of these prices in turn encouraged, especially among
the smaller manufacturers, a considerable degree of speculation in the
purchase of cocoons. On the other hand, with the rapid rise in the
number of manufactories in the 1860s and 1870s, and with the fundamental similarity among all of them of a productive process based primarily
on manual technique, which gave to the large manufactories no advantage
over their smaller rivals in terms of cost and productivity, these fluctuations also made competition in the purchase of cocoons an uncertain
and risky undertaking. The essential instability of this structure of
production, however, was compensated for much of this period by a
general trend of high prices, which even made possible, in certain cases,
the expansion of individual manufactories by direct additions to existing
structures, or by buying out weaker or failed undertakings.

The turning point came in the middle of the 1880s, when prices began to fall on the French market as a result of the reconstruction of the
French cocoon and raw silk producing industry and of the continuing
development of the export production of Japan. As the movement of
lower prices took on the character of a trend, what was required of the
Lebanese manufactories, in order to restore and improve profits, was
the introduction of mechanized equipment and apparatus which would reduce costs by ending their reliance on slower, less productive manual
techniques. In an industry in which accumulation had been slow even
for the larger producers and irregular for the vast majority of smaller
ones, and which could not rely on aid from the paralysed and indebted
Ottoman Government or from organized sources of industrial credit,
those in the best position to make such investments were the merchant
owners of manufactories; but here the essential ambiguity of their position was revealed. In their capacity as industrialists, their interests
lay in the complete technical reorganization of their establishments; in
their capacity as owners or partners of import-export houses, however,
another alternative was available to them. This was to refrain from
expensive and risky investments in new machines and buildings, content-
ing themselves with whatever profit could be made on the basis of the
established process of production, and to employ their capital either in
'surer' areas of this industry, such as advancing money to smaller
manufacturers for the purchase of extra cocoons and raw materials, or
in altogether new spheres of investment either in Lebanese territory

itself, or in other districts of the Ottoman Empire.

It was precisely this pattern which emerged between 1885 and the beginning of the first World War. As the Lyon weaving industry continued to expand and to seek additional sources of provisionment, its interests were served in Lebanon and Syria by a considerable extension of mulberry cultivation and cocoon production. This movement was encouraged from the late 1880s by limited tax exemptions granted to cultivators by the Ottoman Public Debt, a consortium of European shareholders who had obtained the right to collect taxes on much of the agricultural products of the Ottoman Empire, in lieu of the bankrupt Ottoman Government. In the manufacturing spheres, however, what accompanied this movement was not a competitive reorganization of the productive process, a steady elimination of inefficient and speculative producers, and the gradual emergence of a modern, machine-based industry. What occured instead was a rapid increase in the number of smaller manufactories, operating alongside the earlier-established ones, and all on the basis of a similar manual technique; a continuation of the tendency to speculate among the smaller producers and the continuing inability of their larger rivals to eliminate or absorb them; and the almost total subjugation of this productive sector to French and Lebanese banking and merchant interests. The extent of domination by these interests was strikingly clear from the average division of profit which took place between them and the Lebanese owners of manufactories. In the first decade of the 1900s, it was estimated that only one-fifth to one-third of the profit made by manufactories was retained by their owners, the remaining four-fifths to two-thirds going in the form of insurance and freight charges, interest on circulating capital advanced by rural moneylenders and Lyon and Beirut merchant or banking houses, and commissions, fees, and deductions taken by these houses in return for marketing the raw silk.

The oppression and backwardness of these manufactories, moreover, had its parallel in the agricultural sphere, where fundamental changes in mulberry cultivation and silk worm rearing occurred only slowly and haltingly. Mulberry fields owned or acquired by churches and monasteries, Beirut merchants, village usurers and buyers up, and even, to a certain extent, by richer peasant families, continued to be broken up into small parcels and cultivated by peasant metayers or half-croppers, primarily at their own expense; while silk worm rearing took place, as before, in huts or sheds built by these cultivators or in rooms within their own households with materials and implements owned by them. The persistence of this system of small, dispersed productive units was

favoured not only by its cheapness to landowners, but also by the instability of the manufactories themselves, which tended to discourage expensive investments in large, centralized, well-equipped cocoonneries, and
in mulberry cultivation on a larger scale. Its persistence was also
favoured more generally by the limited development of capitalist relations in other areas of manufacturing, which left landowners with little
competition for the services of peasant half-croppers, and kept open a
wide field for the employment of capital by richer village families not so
much in productive activities as in rural trade and usury. This situation was reflected throughout the latter half of the 19th century by the
involvement of a large number of these families - perhaps two or three
times as many, for example, as invested in silk manufactories - in
importing and selling silk worm eggs and buying up silk cocoons for their
resale to manufactories; in moneylending to metayers or to small, independent peasant cultivators; and in village shopkeeping and retail trade -
in imported cloth, vegetables and fruit, grain, sheep and other items.

In the decade and a half preceding the first World War, the depression of the Lebanese economy was evident not only in the falling off of
several of its most important commercial productions, but also in the
growing emigration of peasant families, a movement which had serious-
ly begun in the 1880s and had increased steadily in the following two
decades. Those who disposed of important capital resources, however,
were undertaking to open or extend new fields of investment.   The
Beirut merchants Sirsuq, Salam, and Bayhum obtained a concession from
the Ottoman Government for investment in the agricultural district of
Houle, in northern Palestine; others found investment opportunities in
Egypt. The engineer-industrialist Albert Naqqach, who argued in vain
for a reorganization of the silk industry, was more successful in his re-
commendations for the development of a summer resort season, particularly in villages of the Maten and the Chouf in the mountains above Beirut;
while a member of the merchant family Lahoud, owners of a failed silk
manufactory in Jbayl, was reported to have pressed successive govern-
ments during this period for the opening of a road between this town and
Baalbeck, in the hope of developing the tourist trade and 'stimulating
the economy of Jbayl and its environs.'

In the first years of the 1900s the broad outlines of the Lebanese
economy, as it was to develop for much of the next half century, were
already beginning to emerge in fairly clear form: a weak and limited
manufacturing sphere;   a backward agriculture where capitalist relations penetrated very slowly and where a majority of small cultivators
lived either in debt or in heavy reliance on remittances from emigré re-

latives;   and a pattern of investment in which capital resources were directed largely to non-productive areas, such as import-export, transit and retail trade, rental property and real estate in Beirut, hoteliery, tourism, and land speculation in the Lebanese mountains.   This was the developing direction of the economy over which the French assumed direct control in the aftermath of the first World War.

Selected General References

Chevallier, Dominique   La Société du Mont Liban a l'époque de la Révolution Industrielle en Europe, (Paris, 1971)

Ducousso, Gaston   L'industrie de la soie en Syrie et au Liban (Beirut, 1913)

Guys, Henri   Beyrouth et le Liban: relation d'un séjour de plusieurs années dans ce pays (Paris, 1860)

Haqqi Bey, Ismail   ed.   Lubnan; mabahith ilmiyya wa itjimaiyya (Beirut, 1918);   Edition of Fouad E Boustany (Beirut, 1969)

Sibai, Badr al-Din   Al-rasmal al-ajnabi fi Suriya (Damascus, 1958)

Smilianskaya, I M   al-Harakat al-Fallahiyya fi Lubnan, al-nusf al-awwal min al-qarn al-tasi achar (Beirut, 1972)   (Trans. from the Russian)

Touma, Toufic   Paysans et Institutions féodales chez les Druses et les Maronites du Liban du XVII^C siècle à 1914 (Beirut, 1971)

THE POLITICAL ECONOMY OF GRAND LIBAN, 1920-70

by Roger Owen

The French decision to create a Greater Lebanon (Grand Liban) in 1920 as part of their policy of dividing geographical Syria into a number of smaller states had three important consequences. First, it augmented the pre-dominantly (Maronite) Christian and Druze population of the Mountain – and of the Ottoman sanjak of 1861-1914 - with an almost equally large Muslim population, notably the Sunni town-dwellers of the coastal cities of Tripoli, Beirut and Saida and the Sunni and Shii peasantry of the Akkar plain, the Biqa valley and the south.* The majority of this population had long-standing links with the towns of the Syrian interior and felt no allegiance to the new state, and while the incorporation of the Sunni and Shii leaders into the system of government and administration proceeded more rapidly than is often allowed, the identification of the lower social classes with the new Lebanese entity remain equivocal and they continued to respond readily to political influences from across the borders.

---

*According to the first, inaccurate, census of 1922 there were then 330,000 Christians in Grand Liban, 275,000 Muslims and 43,000 Druze. As for the boundaries no work has yet been done on the reasons why the French fixed them where they did in the north and east (the southern boundary was determined by the frontier with Palestine). It is generally assumed that the French wished to provide the Mountain with access to the adjacent cereal-producing areas in order to make it economically self-sufficient. But it should also be noted that much land in the Biqa valley and on and around the Akkar plain was owned before 1920 by members of powerful Beirut Christian families like the Pharaons and the Eddes.

Second, by deliberately creating a state which was seen as a place of secure refuge for their Christian protegés the French did much to determine the sectarian or confessional character of any new political arrangements.   A system of administration and representation on the basis of religious community was institutionalised in the Constitution of 1926, and although its chief architect, Michel Chiha, might look forward to the day when confessionalism in government would whither away, this was clearly not to be.[1]   Once it was decided to reward the leaders of some of the religious communities with access to high office, and to attempt to incorporate others into the system on the same basis, the French helped to create a powerful pressure group committed to the defence of the existing status quo, something which is well illustrated by the strong opposition to the few tentative efforts by the Mandatory authorities to introduce arrangements of a more secular nature.[2]   Meanwhile, a host of French policies – for example, the distribution of arms to Christian villages in South Lebanon during the Druze/Syrian uprising of 1925/6 – served further to reinforce communal self-consciousness.

Third, by splitting off Grand Liban from its natural hinterland the French not only confirmed the financial and commercial hegemony of Beirut over the Mountain, but also strengthened a pattern of economic activity in which agriculture and industry had become more and more subordinate to banking and trade.   The particular characteristics of this pattern are well-illustrated by the figures for the contribution of the various sectors to National Income in 1950:   agriculture 20 percent, industry (after the Second World War boom) 13.5 percent, trade 28.9 percent.[3]   By contrast Syrian agricultural activity provided roughly half of gnp at the same period.[4]

It was within the space defined by the confessional system of administration and politics, the problems of integrating a large Muslim population, and the dominance of the service sector, as well as by the French presence and French policy, that the characteristic features of the Lebanese political economy developed.   At the centre stood the apparatus of the colonial state, with the gendarmerie, the Chasseurs Libanais, the legal arrangements, designed to maintain order and to secure the French position.   But as in so many other colonial territories there was an important distinction between the power to repress and the lack of the executive power characteristic of the modern state.   In the interests of economy the French kept the number of government officials at a minimum, leaving the bulk of the educational, medical and other services to be provided on a communal basis.   Thus in 1933 there were only 3,600 government servants for a population of nearly 850,000, while in 1938, of the 10,000 pupils in secondary schools only 438 were in government, and hence secular, establishments.[5]

Below the French High Commissioner and his aides stood the Lebanese cabinet and Parliament, the main function of which was to distribute the rewards of office among the different communities. As such they also acted as a magnet for the leaders of those religious groups which it was necessary to integrate into the system, and it was by this means that the non-Maronite Christians, then the Shii notables, and finally some of the leading members of the Sunni community were persuaded of the benefits of cooperation with a separate Lebanese state.[*] In contrast the French hoped to regulate some of the problems raised by the scramble for power and position - for example the built-in tendency to increase government expenditure to provide more jobs - by augmenting the powers of the President in such a way that he might be able to stand above the whole process as some kind of neutral arbiter. But this was not to be: from the mid-1930s onwards the Presidency itself became the object of a fierce struggle between two Maronite factions, those of Emile Edde and Bishara al-Khuri, which from then on placed it at the very centre of the political process.

Meanwhile, outside Parliament and the administration a whole range of confessional leaders both old and new - the Maronite Patriarch, Pierre Gemayal and the para-military Phalange which he formed in 1936, the Muslim Consultative Council formed by a group of Sunni religious notables - attempted to influence policy and to protect their own communal interests by means of the organisation of strikes and demonstrations as well as, on occasions, appeals for support from groups outside Lebanon, such as the Syrian nationalists in Damascus. An understanding of the political role of certain of the Sunni zaims (leaders) in the coastal towns is also important. As Arnold Hottinger notes, the creation of an urban following requires something more than the simple exercise of power and patronage which comes from landownership:

> The zaim of the cities needs political slogans to cement his clientele and to extend his influence beyond the restricted circle of persons who are directly dependent on him.[6]

---

[*] S H Longrigg remarks that by 1936, at the time of the Conference of Coast which passed a strong resolution in favour of transferring Lebanon's Muslim areas back to Syria, it was noted that a number of Sunni notables, including all the members of Parliament, failed to support the pro-Syrian party. Syria and Lebanon under the French Mandate (London, 1958) p219.

In the case of the Karami family of Tripoli or the Salams of Beirut the most powerful and emotive of such slogans were those of Arab nationalism and it was the need to appeal to supporters in this way which defined their political position: they had to maintain their nationalist credentials by standing at some distance from the administration while still being close enough to benefit from some of the rewards which it was able to offer.   This was a complicated balancing act to perform, the more so as in times of crisis, as Hottinger also notes, there was a danger of their becoming prisoners of their own political slogans.[7] This was the case in 1936 when the Sunni zaims could only preserve their leadership by responding to the rising ride of nationalist feeling triggered off by the French attempts to impose new treaty relations on Syria and Lebanon as separate entities.   At these times their skill lay in using such militant displays of feeling to improve their own position and that of their community without doing anything to disrupt the economic and political arrangements of a Grand Liban from which they had already begun to derive great benefit.

A last feature of the Lebanese system as it developed during the Mandate period was the pattern of economic activity.   While what remained of the silk industry was allowed to die off from want of support from the French and from the financiers of Beirut and from the absence of an alternative market to Lyon in the Syrian hinterland, the service sector continued to prosper, assisted by a policy of low tariffs and the creation of an infrastructure of harbours and roads ideally suited to the further expansion of trade, building, and the new business of tourism.

Such in essence were the main charact eristics of a system which by virtue of its confessional political arrangements, its commercially-oriented economy and its underdeveloped government services gave great power to a small class of men, both Christian and Muslim, whose positions as landowners, merchants or bankers was reinforced by the leadership of their respective religious communities.   And it was these same men who, during the Second World War, when temporarily allied against the French, came together to secure their interests in an independent Lebanon on the basis of the unwritten National Pact of 1943。 At one level the compromise which the Pact enshrined involved the final integration of the Sunni bourgeoisie for, in it, they agreed to recognise both the existing borders of Lebanon Lebanon and Christian hegemony within them.   For their part of the bargain the Christian leaders accepted that the newly independent state belonged to the Middle East (i. e. that it was not an outpost of Europe)   and that it should pursue policies which were in harmony with its Arab neighbours.   In so doing they paved the way for easy access to the commercial and financial possibilities of a region in which, among other things, the

export of oil was beginning to assume an increasing importance.[8]   But
above and beyond these considerations, the National Pact also represented an agreement to maintain the economic and political system from
which the leaders themselves derived a double advantage. An extra advantage stemmed from the fact that the maintenance of confessionalism
provided them with an easy way of re-directing any economic discontent:
against their own leadership towards the members of another religious
group.

The years between 1943 and 1958 saw the further consolidation of
the system as well as its first great challenge.   As far as the formal
constitutional arrangements were concerned the situation in this period
is well summed up by a comment of Michael Hudson's on the Presiden-
cies of Bishara al-Khuri (1943-52) and Camille Chamoun (1952-58) that
each of them 'was condemned for being ineffectual and each of them was
condemned for being dictatorial.[9]   Behind this apparent paradox stands
the fact that both Presidents used their office to increase their own power
and that of their associates while doing little to strengthen the structure
of the Lebanese state.   Thus the considerable growth in the number of
government officials under al-Khuri - from under 6,000 in 1947 to
14,800 in 1953 - was largely the result of policies designed to reward
his own political following.[10]   Again, the advance in government spend-
ing under both al-Khuri and Chamoun, while doing something to improve
the country's infrastructure in terms of a new airport and better trans-
port, was also to the benefit of a small group of public works contractors
and ignored the real needs of the people living in the more backward,
rural areas.*   At the same time the size of the army remained small -
6,000 men in 1952, 10,000 in 1956/7 - and there were parts of the country in which taxes were not collected and in which government authority
could hardly be said to have penetrated.[11]

The fact that these were also years of relative political stability owes
much to the economic prosperity of the period, albeit of a very uneven
kind.   Though Lebanon's basic laissez-faire orientation was not finally
confirmed until after the repeal of the Customs Union with Syria in 1950

---

*In 1958 planned government expenditure was still only 13.7 percent
of National Income.   This should be compared with a Syrian figure
of 23.5 percent of gdp in 1960 and a Tunisian one of 20.7 percent for
the same year.   M.D. Hudson, The Precarious Republic: Political
Modernization in Lebanon (New York, 1968) p311;   C.M. Henry, 'The
consolidation and dissipation of power in unincorporated societies:
Egypt and Tunisia' (Mimeo).

(in spite of the protests of the industrial interest) Beirut earlier began to derive great benefit from the closure of Haifa, a major rival, to Arab activity after the establishment of Israel, from the arrival of refugee capital from Palestine, Egypt and elsewhere, and, above all, from its role as an entrepot between Europe and the oil-rich regions of the Gulf.   Between 1950 and 1957 the value of Lebanese commercial activity increased by 56.3 percent and in 1957 itself contributed nearly a third of gnp.[12]

Industry, on the other hand, continued to lag.   Hampered by an over-valued Lebanese pound, by uncertain power supplies, and with little protection from a low external tariff, local entrepreneurs also lacked the political power to persuade the government to come to their assistance. Lebanon was thus deprived of a pressure group which, in other circumstances, would have been able to challenge the hegemony of merchants and bankers whose own interest lay in keeping the power of the state weak. Another result of the slow growth of industry was that the factory labour-force remained small and could not provide the basis for a working class political activity which might have transcended the communal divisions of the urban population.

Equally important, the profits from finance and trade were very unevenly distributed between class and class, region and region, and community and community.   One index of this is that while in 1957 commerce provided almost a third of National Income it employed only twelve percent of the working population.   By contrast agriculture, which contributed only 15.6 per cent of gnp in the same year contained almost half of the labour force.[13]   Furthermore there was widespread corruption affecting both business and government while it has been estimated that the level of tax-avoidance by the larger companies was in the region of 66 2/3 percent.[14] Against this, in agriculture, the major activity of the bulk of the Muslim peasantry, incomes hardly rose at all leading many rural workers to migrate to the towns in search of better-paid employment.   The failure of the government to improve the rudimentaryssystem of social security or to institute development projects in the more backward areas made matters even worse.

Many of the stresses and strains of this period were revealed during the crisis of 1958.   Although the immediate circumstance was the decision of the incumbent President Chamoun to seek another, unconstitutional, term of office at a time of great international tension, mucn of the force behind the opposition to this move came from lower class urban Muslims who felt that their own community, now constituting a majority of the Lebanese population, was being discriminated against and impoverished by the country's wealthy, predominantly Christian, rulers.   But if for

much of 1958 the government virtually ceased to function, if the religious
divisions in the army made military intervention impossible, if order was
only restored after the intervention of an outside power - the United States,
the crisis also revealed as much about the strength of the system as it did
about its weaknesses.   While the leaders of the country's Sunni population,
like Rashid Karami in Tripoli, were forced to take to the streets against
the government as the only way of preserving their control over followers
whose sense of economic and political deprivation was fuelled still further
by the powerful currents of Nasserism and Arabism encouraged by the
union between Syria and Egypt, there is no evidence that they ever planned
to overthrow the existing political arrangements or to attempt to re-unite
the Muslim areas of Lebanon with those across the border.   Proof of this
comes from the fact that the moment the crisis was over and General
Chehab elected President, Karami himself agreed to act as his Prime
Minister.   And it was in this role that he helped to pursue one of the essential features of the new President's policies: the attempt to improve the
political and economic circumstances of the Muslim population, and their
representation in the administration, in such a way as to secure its allegiance more securely to the existing Lebanese state structure.

Apart from his policy towards the Muslims President Chehab't major
efforts were directed at building up the strength of the government apparatus and using this strength to set the state more directly at the centre of
the country's economic and social development.   To this end he brought
a French survey mission to Lebanon;   he established a planning organisation;   he created a Central Bank and instituted some control over Lebanon's
free-for-all banking system.   In addition, he began to prepare a new and
more comprehensive social security law, while increased expenditure on
education meant that during the six years of his Presidency the proportion
of children in government primary and secondary schools increased from
31 to 42 percent.[15]   Just as important, the army - which was expanded to
15,000 men, the police and the new intelligence service - the Deuxième
Bureau, were used to make sure that the authority of the state would be
exercised in all parts of the country.

Taken as a whole this programme of national developments by means
of increased state activity shows a number of similarities with trends in
the surrounding Arab countries.   Thus, by 1964 for example, the government's ordinary and extraordinary expenditure had reached a third of
National Income, almost the same proportion as in Syria.[16]   Nevertheless,
even before the end of his Presidency Chehab was prepared to admit that
'Chehabism' had failed and that the forces of stasis in the system were
too strong for him.   The reasons for this are instructive.   To begin

with, at the root of Chehab's policy there lay a basic contradiction: was
its purpose to strengthen the system or to change it?   This, in turn, implied a number of other important questions: how did a policy of advantag-
ing the Muslims as communities fit in with the attempt to develop secular
'Lebanese' institutions?   Could industry be supported in the teeth of opposition from the bankers and merchants?   Was the only way to undermine
the traditional zaims to encourage rivals from within their own religious
group?   Given the particular nature of Lebanese political and economic
arrangements it was clear that, as the ruling elite regained its power after
1958, it would use it to buttress up its own position and to prevent any further
inroads into it.   This is not to say that President Chehab did not have a
certain success in persuading men like Pierre Gemayal (who joined the
government for the first time) or some of the Sunni notables to play a role
in promoting his policies.   But even such a success was, in an important
sense, counter-productive in that it aroused the fears of other leaders who
believed, rightly, that the increasing strength of the Presidency and of the
state would lead to a diminution of their own power.   For them Chehabism
meant, in part, a direct attack on their position through the extension of
government authority into parts of the country in which they had previously
ruled supreme or through the activities of the Deuxième Bureau in supporting smaller rivals against them.   It also meant, in the longer term, the
establishment of a well-organised civil administration and the extension
of government services in such a way as to reduce their power still further,
by limiting the possibilities of patronage, of offering jobs to their clients
and of providing assistance to the sick and the unemployed whose needs
were virtually ignored by the state.   At the same time the banking and
commercial interests were united in opposing policies which seemed to
them to require an increase in taxation, an opportunity for greater government control over their affairs and, perhaps, the development of an
industrial pressure group which might become powerful enough to challenge
the basic orientation of the economy.

It was for these reasons that, although President Chehab was powerful
enough to chose his own successor as President - Charles Helou (1964-70),
and to bequeath him his own apparatus of 'administration by technocrats, '
supported by the Deuxième Bureau, the army and, externally, by   the
Egyptians, the opposition to Chehabism was now so strong that the experi-
ment soon ground to a halt.   Just how this happened is not easy to discern -
pressure to halt or to divert Chehabist policies was applied so regularly
and consistently by much of the country's economic and political leadership
that it rarely came to the surface in a major confrontation   - but the

results are clear: the corruption and ever more arbitrary activity of
the Deuxième   Bureau, the end of economic planning, the increasing
inefficiency of what few government services existed in many of   the
rural areas.*   The final coup de grace was given by the defeat of the
Chehabist candidate,   Elias Sarkis, in the 1970   struggle   for the Presidency and the election of Sulieman Frangieh on the basis of a specifically
anti-Chehabist (as well as anti-Palestinian) programme.

With the failure of Chehabism the Lebanese state entered a long period
of political and economic crisis in a very weakened condition.   Starting
with the depression that followed the collapse of the Intra Bank in 1966
(itself a reminder of Lebanon's vulnerability to movements and events
beyond its borders) there was then the 1967 Middle East war, the emergence of a strong Palestinian presence inside the country from 1968 onwards, and a long series of damaging Israeli raids.   At the same time
the traditional leadership showed itself as resistant to change as ever
and increasingly unable to accommodate the new forces thrown up by the
cooperation of Left-wing Palestinians with radical Lebanese movements
which were beginning to recruit followers from among the more economically disadvantaged sections of the urban population.   With this the system
of economic and political arrangements institutionalised inside Grand
Liban faced their greatest challenge.

---

* A rare example of such a confrontation occurred after the end of the
   Chehabist period when in September 1971 an attempt to raise customs
   duties on a whole range of imported goods was brought to an end by a
   ten day strike of Beirut merchants and shopkeepers.   The Finance
   Minister, Elias Saba, had originally justified the increase in terms of
   the need to spend more money on economic and social development.   It
   was also supported by the Industrialists' Association which regarded
   the measure as vital for the economy and local industry.   Arab Report
   and Record (1972) p505.

References

1   A H Hourani, 'Ideologies of the Mountain and the City', p38
2   See, for example, S H Longrigg, Syria and Lebenon under the French Mandate (London etc 1958) p150
3   A Y Badre, 'The national income of Lebanon', Middle East Economic Papers (1956) p13;   Lebanon, Ministre du Plan, Besoins et Possibilités de Developpement du Liban: Etude Préliminaire, I, pp77-81
4   IBRD, The Economic Development of Syria (Baltimore 1955) p9
5   M C Hudson, The Precarious Republic: Political Modernization in Lebanon (New York 1968) p311;   Naval Intelligence Division, Syria (April 1943) p187
6   'Zu'ama' in historical perspective' in L Binder (ed) Politics in Lebanon   (New York etc 1966) p96
7   ibid
8   M Johnson, 'Confessionalism and individualism in Lebanon: a critique of Leonard Binder (ed) 'Politics in Lebanon', Review of Middle East Studies, I (1975) p84
9   The Precarious Republic, p262
10 ibid   R E Crow,   'Confessionalism, public administration and efficiency in Lebanon' in Binder, p178
11 Hudson, p312
12 Besoins et Possibilités de Developpement, pp77-81
13 ibid, p87
14 C Issawi, 'Economic development and political liberalism in Lebanon', in Binder, p79
15 Hudson, p322;   C M Henry, 'The consolidation and dissipation of power in unincorporated societies' (Mimeo)
16 Hudson, p312;   Henry

IDEOLOGIES OF THE MOUNTAIN AND THE CITY

by Albert Hourani

In 1963 a group of historians and political scientists held a conference at the University of Chicago to discuss the working of the Lebanese political system, and their papers were later published in a book edited by Leonard Binder, Politics in Lebanon.[1] Anyone who has turned to that book during the last months of civil war in Lebanon, in the hope that it would help him to understand what was happening, must have felt that something had been left out of it.

The idea which seems to have moulded the papers and discussions was that of a self-contained political society seeking and finding its own equilibrium, by a series of successful adjustments to changing circumstances. Throughout the process of change, it was suggested, there could be seen a basic continuity: from the emergence of the 'principality' in the seventeenth and eighteenth centuries, through the various changes in the middle years of the nineteenth, down to the creation of Greater Lebanon in 1920, the Constitution of 1926, the National Pact of 1943, and the reaffirmation of unity after an earlier civil war, that of 1958.

The lessons of this successful process of adjustment seemed clear. For Lebanon to maintain its separate existence, there had to be some kind of authority (that of the prince, the mutasarrif or the president) which, whatever its origins, stood above the interests of particular communities; a habit of discussion and alliance on lines which cut across the frontiers of communities; an agreement on the sharing of power between them; and some measure of agreement also on the purposes for which that power should be used, in particular in relation to the surrounding states.

This analysis may well be valid as far as it goes, and nothing which

has happened in the last few months has disproved it.   It may be however, that the discussions which led to the book, and others like them,
concentrated too much on one problem, that of the balance between
religious communities, and failed to give due importance to other factors which have helped to determine the ways in which the system works
and limit the extent to which it is self-sustaining and can find its own
equilibrium.   Not enough emphasis was laid, for example, on the
smallness and fragility of Lebanon;   it was clear from the time of the
National Pact, or at least from that of the civil war of 1958, that
Lebanon could not easily follow a policy opposed to that of its Arab
neighbours, in regard to the problem of Israel, or that of relations
with the great Powers, but it was not so clear that the surrounding
states would have an interest in making use of any kind of inner fragmentation for their own purposes.   Again, the degree to which the various communities had really been drawn into the political system may
have been exaggerated.   Some groups remained precariously inside or
virtually outside it: the Orthodox Christians, who controlled much of
the wealth of Beirut but played only a minor part in its political life;
the Armenians, who were only marginally involved in it;   the Shi^{c}is,
who had been formally drawn in by being given the third office of state,
that of the President of the Chamber, but who had needs and aspirations
which were only just beginning to be formulated;   above all, the Palestinians, who scarcely existed as a separate political force in 1963.

Perhaps the most important factor which was not so clear then as
it is now is that the 'communities' are not, beyond a certain limit,
solid bodies having a single interest or attitude, and the division into
religious communities is not the only division which can be made of the
population of Lebanon, and in some ways may not be the most significant.   We can now see that it is necessary to ask, exactly who in each
community profits from the position it has in the political system?   In
general, it would be true to say that those who have profited have been,
on one level, the commercial and financial groups whose interests have
been served by the policy of openness to the outside world which was
implicit in the 'National Pact', and that of laissez faire in internal
matters which was implicit in the agreement that government should be
carried on by a balancing of interests between the various communities;
and on another, the political leaders, to whom the system, based as it
was on a process of bargains and alliances at the top, guaranteed the
exercise of patronage and thus the possibility of maintaining their own
systems of clients.   By and large, there was close agreement between
the interests of the leaders and those of the commercial and financial

class, and this became more significant and dangerous as the economic
and social system changed, first with the growth of Beirut and the extension of its power over the hinterland, and then, in the last few years,
with the growth in and around Beirut of a depressed world of rural immigrants and Palestinian refugees, not sharing in the profits of trade
and finance and affected by inflation.

The solidarity of each community was exaggerated, and so too therefore was the extent to which it had accepted the Lebanese political system.
If there was a basic agreement amongst most of the leaders about the
way in which the system should work, this did not necessarily mean that
there was deeper or wider agreement about the nature of Lebanon or the
purposes for which its political system should be used, or, in other words,
that there really existed a Lebanese political society.

Much of the political writing about Lebanon seems to assume that
the history of Lebanon has been that of the gradual expansion of the political tradition of the Christian parts of the Mountain, and the gradual
conversion of Druzes, Sunnis and Shi^{C}is to a political idea which had
grown up among the Maronites.   What happened in fact, however, was
different;   it was a broadening agreement between political elites, each
of which controlled its community in its own way and in the name of its
own political ideologies.   To the extent to which they entered the Lebanese
political alliance, they did so with their own modes of action and their
own traditions.

It has been customary to refer to the heads of these elites as za^{C}im's,[2]
but this term covers at least three different modes of political activity.
First, there is the 'feudal' mode: that of the great lords of those parts
of the countryside where large estates and traditional lordships exist
(among Druzes and Shi^{C}is in the south, Shi^{C}is in the Biqa^C, and Sunnis
in ^{C}Akkar).   Their power rests on their position as landowners, often
of ancient lineage, their use of strong-arm men, and their ability to
give protection and patronage.   Secondly, there are the 'populist' politicians of the mainly Christian regions in the northern half of the country,
where smallholdings are common, and leadership has less of a solid
base of socio-economic power, and is derived on the one hand from the
use of powers of protection and patronage to maintain political 'clans',
on the other from some kind of ideology or programme of action.
Thirdly, there are the leaders of the Muslim populations of the coastal
cities;   they also obtain and retain leadership by ideological appeal
and the exercise of patronage, but add to these a third source of power,
the manipulation of the urban masses, mobilised for them by the 'strong
arm' men of the popular quarters, the qabadai's.[3]

Of these three kinds of leader, therefore, two have to appeal in terms of ideologies and programmes, and cannot simply rely on primordial loyalties or allegiances.   It is here that the differences between the political traditions which have come together to form Lebanon are relevant.   We can distinguish two broad groups of ideologists, which we may call those of the mountain and those of the city, and within each of them a number of sub-divisions can be made.

The 'ideologies of the mountain' are specifically ideologies of the Maronite community.   They have at least three aspects, connected with different phases in the history of the Maronites.[4]   The idea which emerged earliest was that of a compact community, the Maronite church, living by itself under its own hierarchy, protecting itself from attack by the Muslim rulers of the cities and plains, and also against the more insidious attacks of Jacobites and other 'heretics'.   This idea is already present in the histories of the Patriarch Istifan Duwaihi in the seventeenth century, and forms a permanent strand in Maronite self-consciousness..   Maronites are aware of themselves as the only Catholic 'nation' in the Near East, and indeed of Asia, and are therefore sensitive to any doubts cast on their Catholicism;   the idea of the 'perpetual orthodoxy' of the Maronites, and Leo X's description of them as 'a rose among thorns', have been themes of Maronite writers. At the same time, however, they have strongly defended their position as a Uniate Church against encroachments by Rome;   the failure of the Catholic church as a whole to canonize some whom the Maronites accept as saints has also been a theme of Maronite writing.

At a rather later stage a second idea emerged, that of this 'nation' as living within a broader political framework, that established and maintained by a hierarchy of leading families, associated with each other as a political élite.   Implicit in this idea was a certain religious pluralism, for the leading families were Sunni, Druze and Maronite, and the alliances between them cut across religious divisions.   This idea can be found, explicitly or by implication, in the work of some historians of the nineteenth century, such as Haidar Shihab and Tannus Shidiaq.   It could scarcely have emerged earlier, because it was only in the eighteenth century that the northern, mainly Maronite, parts of the mountain were absorbed into the area controlled by the prince, and only in the later part of that century that the dominant section of the princely family of Shihab became Maronite and so provided a focus for Christian loyalty.

After the abolition of the princedom in the 1840s there began a campaign, supported by France, for the restoration of a Maronite Shihab.

In the work of a political writer of the time, Nicolas Murad, we can see
both these ideas present: the Maronites are a separate religious group,
a perpetually orthodox part of the Catholic church, but they are also
ethnically distinct, descendants of the 'Mardaites', a mysterious people
mentioned in the history of the early Islamic period.   From this time
onwards there is an attempt to give historical depth to the idea of a separate and virtually independent political entity.   Emphasis is placed
upon the role of the Druze prince of the seventeenth century, Fakhr al-
Din II, as the creator both of Lebanese independence and of the principle
of communal alliance.   This idea owes much to the historical work of
the Maronite Bulus Qar'ali, but has been given full expression by another
historian, ᶜAdil Ismaᶜil, a Sunni from one of the few Sunni villages in
the mountain. [5]

In the troubled years of the mid-nineteenth century a third
strand appears, that of 'populism', a new kind of appeal made by a new
kind of claimant to leadership.   Such an appeal could be made in the
Christian villages of the north more easily than in the east or south.
The northern part of the mountain had not had a highly developed 'feudal'
structure, because since Mamluk and early Ottoman times it had been
under more direct control by a governor of Tripoli;   further south, in
Kisrawan, there was a lordly family, that of Khazin, but the small cultivators had been able to throw off its domination in a popular movement
encouraged by the Church;   to the south and east, there were mainly
Christian market towns of recent growth - Zahle and Dair al-Qamar -
which had grown up in regions dominated by Druze lords but were re-
luctant to accept their control.   In all these regions, Christians in
villages and small towns were open to the appeal of 'populist' leaders:
Tanious Shahin who led the little revolt of Kisrawan, Yusuf Karam who
led the forlorn hope of the Maronites against the compromises involved
in the Organic Law of 1861-4, and the members of the Administrative
Council who opposed attempts by the mutasarrif to limit the special privileges granted in the Organic Law of 1861.   In a sense, the Phalanges
of to-day can be seen as the heirs of this tradition.

Implicit in this mountain populism was a certain distrust of the city,
an expression of that tension between countrymen and city-dwellers
which has been described by Baroja as one of the 'ancient commonplaces' of Mediterranean society. [6]   For the villager, rural society is
created by God, urban by man;   the life of the fields is 'natural' life
in all its purity.   This image of a pure and natural way of living was
carried by the emigrants to the cities of the New World, strengthened
and perhaps distorted there by nostalgia, and reflected back from them

onto Lebanon itself.

The Lebanon of the eighteenth and nineteenth centuries did not include the larger towns of the coast.   Lebanese claims and French policy led to their incorporation into 'Greater Lebanon' in 1920, and in the next half century one of them, Beirut, became a great centre of international trade and finance, of services and communications.   It became not only a part but the dominant part of the country, and from it there came other ideas of what Lebanon was or should be.   Implicitly or explicitly, the urban idea of Lebanon was neither of a society closed against the out-side world, nor of a unitary society in which smaller communities were dissolved, but something between the two: a plural society in which communities, still different on the level of inherited religious loyalties and intimate family ties, co-existed within a common framework.

This idea begins to emerge in the second half of the nineteenth cen-tury, partly as a reaction to the civil troubles of 1860, partly as a reflection of the policy of the Tanzimat in the Ottoman Empire as a whole, but basically as the expression of the interests of a commercial city, where men must meet in peace and order to do business, and doors should be open to the outside world.   It was this idea, rather than those of the mountain, which guided the political development of Lebanon from 1920 onwards, that is to say, from the time when Beirut was incorporated in it.

There was more than one way, however, in which it could be express-ed and explained.   On the one hand, the idea of a plural Lebanon could be a kind of transplantation and modification in the city of the idea of the Christian mountain.   This can be seen in the writings of Michel Chiha, who was not only a theorist of Lebanese nationalism but one of its creators, for he played a large part in drafting the constitution of 1926.[7]   His writing is Christian in its cultural content rather than its explicit ideas.   His ideal is that of a pluralist and non-sectarian state, and he accepts communalism with reluctance, and as a temporary exped-ient: in the words of the Constitution, it should be accepted à titre transitoire.   When he writes about Palestine there is an Arab element in what he says, which is far from the strict neutralism of the Maronite mountain, and is perhaps connected with his acceptance of the weak-ness of Lebanon and its need to lie open to the world around it;   the Lebanese are 'by vocation and necessity, the friends of the masters of the world'.   At this point however the essential tension of Lebanon's existence appears: 'we are not disposed to resign ourselves to the decline of Europe'.   Between Arab and European affinities, the tension can only be resolved in a concept which can include them both, that of

a common 'Mediterranean civilization', the source of all belief in a
supernatural world. [8]

A more extreme and less influential version of a similar idea was
put forward in the same period by a number of men of letters, and by
Charles Corm in particular.   Lebanon is seen as the heir of Phoenicia.
The modern Lebanese are descendants of the Phoenicians.   Their distinctive culture, although expressed in modern languages and styles,
reveals 'the atavistic forms of the national sensibility'.   Like Phoenicia,
Lebanon is part of the world of classical Mediterranean civilization and
can only live by immersion in it.   But this vision is suffused with a
Maronite romanticism;   Lebanon is not only the heir of Phoenicia, it
is the child of the Church, the only Christian country in Asia. [9]

There was however a second type of urban conception of Lebanon,
not a transplantation of the ideas of the mountain, but a transplantation
of later Ottoman ideas.   For those Muslims who, in the 1930's and
1940's, came to accept the existence of Lebanon, it was an embodiment
of the ideal formulated, in different ways, by the statesmen of the
Tanzimat and their Syrian supporters, and then by the Ottoman liberals
and their allies in the Arab cities, the Party of Decentralization and
the Beirut Reform Committee of 1913.   It should be carefully non-
sectarian, with a national concept embracing all but suffused with a
memory of the Arab, and therefore the Muslim, past.   Lebanon should
be a separate part of a broader unity, conceived not in terms of classical Mediterranean classical civilization but of that of the Arabs. [10]
(A variation of this idea was that put forward by the Hizb al-Qawmi,
the Parti Populaire Syrien, in the 1930's, the idea of a territorially
limited and strictly non-sectarian Syrian nation, child of another late
Ottoman idea, current in Beirut towards the end of the nineteenth
century, carried from there to the emigrant community in Brazil and
brought back to Lebanon by the son of an emigrant.   Although it had a
special appeal to some Lebanese, in particular those who were neither
Maronite nor Sunni Muslim, it was by its nature an idea which challenged the separate existence of Lebanon, not one which underpinned it.) [11]

It was such urban ideas which formed, so to speak, the 'official'
ideological basis of the Lebanese state.   The events of recent months
have shown how fragile that basis was.   In political terms, it laid its
main emphasis on the institution of the Presidency, standing above
religious communities and political 'clans', and on the possibility of
an alliance between Maronite and Sunni leaders (one of the first Sunnis
to accept the existence of Lebanon, Khair al-Din Ahdab, stated in 1932
that 'we demand the Presidency for the Muslims or the Maronites, to

the exclusion of the minorities').[12]   In terms of social forces, it assumed that the common interest of the commercial and financial classes would give strength to this alliance.   But the Presidency could never liberate itself from political clans, and, at moments of deep division between communities, it could not easily stand aside.   The alliance of Christian and Muslim politicians did not necessarily imply a merging of the communities in whose names they spoke;   on the contrary, the new immigrants into the cities seemed to be more conscious of sectarian differences than those living in the countryside.[13]   What is most important, the civil war has shown how much of Lebanon has not been fully drawn into the political community: the Sunni urban leaders can no longer speak in the name of the Muslim part of the population; and in the Maronite organizations we can see the expression of a community never fully at home in Beirut, still rooted in the villages, uneasy with the compromises of the political system, appealing against the ideologies of the city to those of the Maronite mountain.

References

1   L Binder (ed.), Politics in Lebanon (New York etc. 1966);   see also M Hudson, The Precarious Republic: Political Modernization in Lebanon (New York, 1968) and K S Salibi, The Modern History of Lebanon (London, 1965)

2   A Hottinger, 'Zuᶜama in historical perspective' in Binder, p. 85f

3   A Blok, The Mafia of a Sicilian Village 1860-1960 (Oxford, 1974)

4   I F Harik, Politics and Change in a Traditional Society: Lebanon, 1711-1845 (Princeton, 1968);   K S Salibi, Maronite Historians of Mediaeval Lebanon (Beirut, 1959);   Salibi, 'The Traditional historiography of the Maronites' in B Lewis and P M Holt (ed.), Historians of the Middle East (London etc. 1962), p. 212f; A H Hourani, 'Historians of Lebanon' in Lewis and Holt, p. 226f

5   P Carali (B Qar'ali), Fakhr al-Din II .... al Corto di Toscana (Rome, 1936) and Fakhr al-Din al-Maᶜni al-thani (Harissa, 1938); A Ismail, Histoire du Liban, vol I, Le Liban au temps de Fakhr al-Din II (1590-1633) (Paris, 1955)

6   J C Baroja, 'The city and the country: reflexions on some ancient commonplaces' in J Pitt-Rivers (ed.), Mediterranean Countrymen (Paris etc, 1963)

7   P Rondot, 'The political institutions of Lebanese democracy' in Binder, p. 127f

8   M Chiha, Essais, 2 vols (Beirut, 1950-52), particularly vol I, p. 202 and vol II, p. 200;   A Hourani, Arabic Thought in the Liberal Age (London etc. 1962), p. 319f

9   C Corm, L'art phénicien: petit répertoire (Beirut, n. d), p. xxxix

10   E E Ramsaur, The Young Turks: Prelude to the Revolution of
     1908 (Princeton, 1957);   R I Khalidi, The Development of
     British Policy towards Syria and Arab Nationalism, 1906-1914
     (DPhil thesis, Oxford, 1974), chaps 4 and 5

11   L Zuwiyya Yamak, The Syrian Social Nationalist Party: an
     Ideological Analysis (Cambridge, Mass 1966)

12   Rondot in Binder, p136

13   F I Khuri, 'Sectarian loyalty among rural immigrants in two
     Lebanese suburbs: a stage between national and family
     allegiance' in R Antoun and I Harik, Rural Politics and Social
     Changes in the Middle East (Bloomington etc 1972), p198f

'THE PHALANGE AND THE MARONITE COMMUNITY':
FROM LEBANONISM TO MARONITISM

by Tewfik Khalaf

'The Maronite community's history is a continuous
struggle to maintain national and religious identity
in a dominant Moslem environment.'
Istfan al-Duwayhi (1629-1704)

The following paper is concerned with contributing to a better understanding of the Lebanese Phalange party and the community of which it is the
main striking force - the Maronites. Since the present crisis broke out
in March 1975 the struggle has been presented in the media as one between
under-privileged leftist Moslems and the Maronite community, clinging
to its privileges. Intellectuals and journalists have made great play with
the idea of a 'belt of misery' which the Moslems and Palestinians have
formed around the prosperous city of Beirut. But such accounts never
take into consideration 'another belt upon which this 'belt of misery' was
superimposed: the belt inhabited by the Maronites of Sin-el-Fil, Hadath,
Dekwaneh, Karm-el-Zaytoun, Siufi, Furn-el-Chebbak, Ain-el-Remaneh
and Haret-Horeik. These areas too were inhabited by people who had to
leave their villages to seek work in Beirut: these people too were victims
of the centripetal economy of the country which made the whole of Lebanon
a 'belt of misery' round Beirut. It is also often stated that the Maronites
have monopolised the state and its resources for their sole benefit.

Again, it is not the purpose of this paper to affirm or to deny allegations of this kind, even if such a thing could be done without a proper study of the benefits in money or employment or in development projects resulting from the various government offices which were held by members of the various communities.   Much more important than an examination of the relationship of the Maronite community to the state or to other communities, it is my belief that the key to the understanding of the present crisis, and especially of its escalation, lies in an analysis of relations within the Maronite community.

Without going into the details of the Lebanese experience, we may safely say that, until recently, the original compromise of 1943 has worked quite smoothly: with the ruling groups collecting substantial material benefits some of which were then redistributed to the lower classes through the traditional Lebanese policy of 'eating and feeding'.   As a journalist wrote recently, the country was run as a company. But as the profits of this 'company' began to decline with the recession that followed the crash of the Intra-Bank in 1966 the remainder was increasingly monopolised by the ruling groups while the lower stratas of the Moslem communities began to escape more and more from their traditional leadership.

However, there was more to it than recession. In fact you could say that it is economic development itself which is mainly responsible for the present crisis. Since 1943, in the process of building up a profitable country and in the search for a new Lebanese supra-community identity, the Sunni and Shi'a leaders have grown more and more Lebanese, less and less Moslem;   and this at a time when, in the Arab world as a whole, both the generation and the social classes which the Karamis, the Salams and the As'ads represent, were being supplanted in the hearts and feelings of the Arab masses by new figures and new groups - Nasser, the military state, the 'state bourgeoisie', and the Palestinian movement.   Therefore, for the Lebanese Moslem, the ultimate reference lay outside his local, traditional leadership.   This led to a destructuring of the Moslem communities and to a beginning of their restructuring via the leftist and nationalist parties and via the Palestinian organisations.   It was just because the Moslem leaders agreed to play the game of modernity and to gamble on the progress of the Lebanese experience that they lost control of their 'street'.

But while the Moslems' newly-found 'Lebanonism' entailed a bypassing of their Arab and Moslem loyalties - especially when Arabism and Islamism acquired a socialist connotation - the Maronites Lebanonism was still based on the Maronite identity, aspirations, and structures.   Maronite Lebanonism in 1975 was Lebanonism of 1920,

i.e. Maronitism.* And this Maronitism entailed a very precise political behaviour on behalf of the leaders who were actually prisoners of
their 'street'. Their margin of manoeuvre, and the social and economic
intercourse they entertained with the Moslems and the Arab world were
limited by two kinds of considerations: (a) at an ideological level, the
Maronites had to feel, constantly, that Lebanon was still theirs; (b) at
an economic level, the profits generated by such an intercourse had
to benefit the leaders' families, relations, villages, regions and community. The inner structures of the community (extended family, patron-
client relations, emigre groups, extensive religious educational system)
have maintained the tradition of solidarity.   And in this respect, the
Phalange party has played a great role in establishing patronage relation
and offering services (khadamat) on a supra-family, supra-zaim, supra-
regional basis, in other words, on a true communal basis, thus increasing
tremendously the cohesion of the community. While in the Shi'a community for example the Lebanese Communist Party aimed at breaking the
relation of the peasant to his lord and replacing it by a politically-minded,
challenging, revolutionary relation with the Party, directed against the
Lebanese system, the Phalange Party, by supplanting the local notables,
kept on fulfilling his traditional functions, but at a much higher level of
efficiency and organization. The Communist Party had a revolutionary
and de-structuring effect on the Shi'a, while the Phalange helped the Maronite to maximize his interests and aspirations within the existing system.
And here it would be interesting to point out that the three most homogeneous communities have at their disposal three strong parties: the Phalange
for the Maronites, the PSP for the Druze and the Tashnag for the Armenians.

The Maronite leadership has managed to maintain the cohesion of the
community by: (a) cultivating the traditional solidarity of this sect which
is mainly composed of a middle class people and independent peasants;
(b) maintaining its implicit ideology - individualism and anti-State attitudes,
western orientations, and fear of the Moslem sea around Lebanon;   and
(c) redistributing quite fairly, within the community, the piece of cake
allotted to it by the system. While the Moslem aristocracy and

---

* I Harik writes that the Maronites constitute a national group reflecting
  'distinctive ethnic characteristics, a single religion, and a long
  history; for centuries they lived in one compact area and once had a
  distinct language (of which they kept some vestiges in their religious
  books) and memories up to the recent past'. (1)

bourgeoisie parted with the Arabist and Socialist aspirations of the Moslem masses and felt closer to the Westernized Christian elites, the Maronite leaders had, or successfully pretended to have, more affinities with the Maronites of lower social status than they would with their Moslem counterparts. We may say that even when the rich Maronite accepted the rich Moslem socially, he nonetheless segregated against him culturally. As a result, the poorest of the Maronites felt closer to his leaders than to the poor Moslems. Thus, the Maronites of the low social classes were driven into an accepted alliance with the Maronite upper classes, and through the latter, into an alliance - reluctantly recognized or accepted - with the ruling groups as a whole.

The Maronite common man felt very different from the Moslem. He never did like him. He seemed to tolerate him; but in fact he did not tolerate him as much as he ignored him. And he could ignore him as long as this Moslem did not threaten to challenge his factual, or imaginary position of dominance. Moreover, this Maronite probably felt that as long as he did not feel threatened, the Moslems, within and without Lebanon, were important for his self-identification at a religious, cultural and social level: the rival minaret emphasized the importance of the belfry; the bells answered the Allah Akbar; the defeat of the Arab armies at the hand of Israel strengthened his identification with the West; the mediocrity of governmental and Makassed schools enhanced the superiority of his own religious educational system; the Moslem slum areas contrasted against his neat and comfortable petit-bourgeois world; the challenge set up by the Left and the PLO to the traditional Moslem leadership increased the attachment of his leaders to him. His opposition to Islam and Communism led him to oppose Arabism in its Islamic and anti-Western varieties. 'Pays phénicien, hellenisé, romanisé, croisé, chrétien, tout ce qu'on veut, mais pas pays arabe ... rêvant parfois encore, s'ils n'osent plus en parler, au bastion sionisto-chrétien appuyé à la Mediteranée contre le déferlement de la poussée arabo-musulmane".[2] And who hasn't heard this old Maronite and Christian adage: 'Once they have finished with Saturday (the Jews), they will attack Sunday'. Lebanon is seen 'not so much as the western frontier of the Arab east but as the eastern frontier of the Christian West'.[3]

What has just been described may be defined as the Maronites' ethical world-view and belief system, as John Entelis calls it.[4] To what extent does the Phalange Party espouse such a view? We may distinguish three phases in the evolution of the Party. During the first phase (1936-43) the Phalange Party 'is neither for, nor against anyone. It is for Lebanon' (Shaykh Pierre Gemayel). In 1938 it was defined as a 'purely Lebanese institution free of any confessional or racial characteristics, fighting against all anti-nationalist doctrines which seek to destroy or diminish present-day Lebanon. The Phalange Party is for an ordered and disciplined democracy. Its motto is: God, Fatherland, Family.' During this period, the Phalange movement was characterized by a fanatical attachment to the concept of an independent Lebanon, of which Maronite nationalism was the significant motivating force. At the level of organization it was a militia-based autocratic centralism.

In the second phase, after independence, the Phalange became involved in politics in order to counter the activities of the PPS and the pan-Arabists. In 1952 the Party was defined as Lebanese social-democratic, and at the level of organization it was characterized by a diluted form of autocratism, with the newly established section (qism)competing with the military unit (firqah) as the basic organizational entity. The same year, democratic centralism replaced autocratic centralism, and the social cell (khaliyya) became the third basic unit of the party's organization. Finally, after 1958, the party overtly accepted interconfessionalism as an integral part of the Lebanese nationalist concept. As the Moslem elites were growing in their attachment to the Lebanese entity, the Party, by establishing an alliance with them, had agreed to liberalize its ideology and to accept a more Arab Lebanon in exchange for prosperity. This lead the party to gradually discard its original dogmatism and to espouse a more liberal philosophy. By 1966, the individual had officially replaced the family as the basic operative unit in the Phalange's view of society; and Antoine Najm, the party's idealogue, could then say:
'The Phalange cannot conciliate a totalistic view of life with liberty of the individual. While man is essentially social, he transcends society, for he has a value in and for himself.'[5]
Entelis saw in this process the transformation of a proto-fascist clique into an inter-confessional, nationwide party aiming at creating a European-style democracy. Such a statement however, completely disregards the nature of the Lebanese socio-economic formation and its limitation. It is true that the party has broadened its cross-confessional basis, but its adherents' aspirations were in no way directed towards the construction of a modern and democratic state (in the Western sense of the word) but rather at the maximization of their own short-term interests within the existing 'Multi-state system'. The Phalange did replace many of the old regional and clanic notables, but it continued to fulfil their traditional functions. Instead of courting a notable who could be in dis-

grace tomorrow, people were attracted towards the Phalange party which could insure employment, government offices, import licences, building licences, etc.   Backed by powerful financial lobbies and, more important-ly, by a huge nationwide basis (or if you wish, clientele), mobilized through the multitude of 'Houses of the Phalange' (Bayt al-Kataib), the Party appeared like a highly organized, permanent notable.   If one dis-regards this aspect of the Phalange one cannot understand why, since April 1975, the Party has constantly taken a communal rather than a class position.

Until the 1950's the Phalange attachment to the Lebanese entity was very vague in content, as is the case with all Maronites who want an inde-pendent, sovereign western orientated, Christian dominated Lebanon. But all this is neither clear nor precise.   When P. Gemayel declared: 'We are not for, nor against anyone.   We are for Lebanon,' he was demonstrating a rather poor political vision;   and certainly not defending class interests.   But by the end of the 50's, the Phalange's view of the Lebanese entity had become much more precise.   Once the party had equated the vague concept of Lebanese entity with a specific form of socio-economic formation, it started looking for allies and foes in relation to this socio-economic formation it was now defending.   After 1958, but especially after 1967, the Phalange was to build a 'natural' though not admitted alliance between the ruling groups, i.e. people who are attached to a specific socio-economic form of Lebanon, and the Maronite community as a whole, i.e. people who are attached to a vague definition of Lebanon. J Entelis writes that 'Post-1958 pressures, especially from Masserite, pan-Arabist, Ba'thist, and Palestinian guerrilla forces, necessitated the employment of a modern political instrument that could take direct action on behalf of the system.   Such was the role of the Phalange after 1958.'[6] In other words, the system was in need of an effective repressive instru-ment which would not be bound by ideological considerations.   While the Lebanese (and Arab) 'State' could not repress the Palestinians without bringing discredit on the Moslem elite and endangering their crumbling position, the Phalange could act as the instrument of the ruling groups in repressing any challenge to the status quo, and at the same time, by doing so, act according to the belief system of the average maronite.   It is this coincidence between the requirements of the ruling groups and the aspirations of the Maronite community which constituted the real strength of the Phalange.   And it is when this convergence of interests vanished, in April 1975, that the Party had to make a choice.

From 1967 until 1975, the intransigeant attitude of the Maronite leader-ship was aimed at counterbalancing the impotance of the Moslem part of

the ruling class which had been ideologically paralyzed by the emotional
rise of Arab nationalism.[7] The famous Treaty of Cairo (1969) which
consecrated the strength of the Palestinians in Lebanon was seen in many
Maronite mileux as a capitulation, and new groups emerged which were
dissatisfied with the Maronite leadership's involvement with the Moslems,
or rather with its consequence - an increasingly Arab Lebanon.   And
whilst the Phalange's attitude towards the Palestinians reflected as much
the interests of the ruling groups as the aspirations of the average
Maronite, the reaction of these extreme-right wing groups to the same
phenomenum reflected what we may call the 'petty ideology' of the
Maronites.   Whilst the Phalange's Discourse * was seen by most
Phalangist leaders, by the Moslem elite, the Left, and the Palestinians,
as a 'veil' masking group interest, the extreme-right wing held the same
kind of Discourse for the sake of the Discourse.   Their Discourse was
both form and essence at the same time.   It meant what it said and
nothing more.   They resented the Palestinians as a new community of
Moslems, their 'State within the State,' the Palestinian road-blocks etc.
They were afraid of the slide of Lebanon into the arms of the Arab world;
they were even afraid of the growing economic ties of the country with
the Arabs.   Although of well-to-do families, they felt closer to the
Maronite peasant than to the Moslem bourgeois;   they put family, community, pride and honour above economic interests and class solidarity. In
fact they rejected the concept of class solidarity just as they rejected the
concept of class struggle.   When they engaged in lucrutive activities,
their profits were meant to serve in enhancing their position before their
family, their region and their community.   In their eyes, capital does
not bear the same significance as it does in a modern state;   it is merely
a means sought to achieve a position within their parochial milieu,   to
establish themselves as a notable, to be regarded as the benefactors of
the family.   Money is a source of prestige and not a means to amass more
money.

---

* By Discourse I mean the totality of Phalangist doctrines, political
   philosophies, world-views, statements, published material, pamphlets,
   slogans, and mobilizing incentives used by the Party since 1936,
   together with the programmes of political education diffused in the
   various cells, sections and 'Houses' of the Party, mainly for the benefit of the average Maronitists or Lebanist,   and ranging from the
   motto of the Party - God, Fatherland, Family - to declarations on
   behalf of a distinct Lebanese identity

While the Moslem elites grew in their attachment to the Lebanese socio-economic formation, these pre-capitalist, irrational (in the modern European sense of the word) Maronites did not hesitate to challenge the entire system. Their attachment to the Lebanese entity as they saw it lead them to threaten the Lebanese socio-economic formation. Their resentment grew with the impotence of the 'State' to subdue the Palestinians once and for all. Since the Treaty of Cairo, and especially since the events of May 1973, the Phalange, the Defenders of the Cedar, the Front for the Defence of the Mountain, the Zghoriot Liberation Army, have been preparing for a showdown with the Palestinians - a defensive form of preparation, as they believed that the bulk of the job would be done by 'their State' and 'their Army.' However, when the Army intervened in Saida, in March 1975, against the Left backed by the Palestinians, the Communists and the Nasserites were swift to denounce its partisan role and its predominantly Christian character, thus discrediting it and reducing its room for manoeuvre. But the coup de grace was given to the Army the next day, when tens of thousands of Christians demonstrated in the Christian districts of Beirut in its support. This move seemed to underline the campaign led by the Left and it paralyzed the Army completely. These events constitute a turning point in the Lebanese crisis. When fighting broke out in April between the Phalange and the Palestinians, the right-wingers' aim was to hold on for a few days and then engage the Army in a Jordanian-style campaign against the Palestinians. But the Phalange had underestimated the political gains which the Left had made in Saida: the Army was discredited in the eyes of the Moslem street, and the Left quickly entered the battle so that an intervention by the Army would bee seen as an attack against the Shi'a Lebanese and not against Palestinians.

The struggle against the Left and the Palestinians had major consequences for the evolution of the Phalange Party: it consecrated the predominance of the military firqah over the civilian qism and khaliyya, and it lead the party to seek the assistance of 'maximalist' elements such as retired Army officers, Defenders of the Cedars, Kesrwanee Front, Rahbaniyya Marouniyya, and emigré groups. Henceforth, the Phalange Party would become increasingly a prisoner of its own Discourse. To counter the impotence of the State the party had to mobilize the Maronites by showing them that the Discourse it held was not a mere veil. All this strengthened the position of extremist elements within the community. Faced with the choice between a class position and a communal position, the Phalanges Party was led to make the second choice.

Different factors determined this choice: the absence of a homo-

geneous ruling class propounding a dominant national ideology; * the
peculiar nature of the Lebanese state; the crumbling position of the old
Moslem leadership; the intransigeant position of the Left which was asking for the political isolation ('azl) of the Party; the short-term investment made by the economic elites; and the absence of an infrastructure
to be protected at all costs - roads, railways, dams, factories, machin-
ery, etc.** As the State and the ruling groups could not play the role
which the Maronites were expecting them to play, it meant the end of the
'natural' alliance of the Maronite community with these groups. This
constituted a major change in the attitude of the Maronites vis à vis the
Lebanese system and entity. Here we may point out a very grave analyti-
cal error on behalf of the Left which was asking for the isolation of the
Phalange and was refusing to enter any government in which the party
would be represented. For the Left was thinking of the Phalange in pre-
1975 terms, i.e. Phalange equals instrument of the ruling groups. It
did not understand that by May 1975 the party was closely identified with
the Maronite community - once the bridges linking it to the Moslem elites
had been pulled down - and that the demand for the isolation of the
Phalanges amounted to a demand for the isolation of the Maronite community.

After the first round of fighting in June 1975, three Maronite dele-
gations left Beirut for Paris, Washington and the Vatican. In Paris, the
Maronites were told by Jacques Chirac that France's close relations
with the Arabs did not allow for a pro-Maronite 'prise de position'. In
Washington, a delegation representing the Maronite Monks (Rahbaniyya
Maruniyya) was told that a US landing similar to that of 1958 would have
negative counter-effects and that the US would oppose any move for
partition. In the Vatican, a delegation headed by Amin Gemayel heard
the same story. The Pope opposed partition, and so did Bkiri (the

---

* We can only speak of a juxtaposition of ruling groups whose interests
were not necessarily identical in all circumstances.

** All through the civil war which would have bankrupted any 'sound'
economy, the Lebanese pound has stood firm on all currency markets.
In spite of the gradual destruction of the country, the Service Economy -
at an international level - has kept on going and flourishing from other
places - Amman, Athens - where most Lebanese and Lebanese-based
banks, firms and capitals have taken refuge. This goes on to prove
that Lebanon was only important as a head-office, and could
explain why the powerful financial lobbies gave in without a fight and
surrendered the country to anti-capitalist forces on all sides.

Patriarchate) and the majority of Maronite bishops, as this would en-
danger the position of eight million Christians living in the Arab world.
On the other hand, as far as the advocates of partition were concerned:

> 'the part should not disappear for the sake of the whole – especially
> when this part represents quality and not quantity.   And what is
> more, the other Christians involved are not even Maronites.   If
> they were offered the choice between liberty and social justice, the
> Maronites would choose liberty, even if this means separation from
> Rome.'[8]

On November 15 1975 Shaykh Pierre Gemayel declared to Al-Safir:
'Social justice exists only in heaven.'   This was not an elitist statement.
Shaykh Pierre was only expressing his belief that the inner structures
of the Maronite community – family, patronage, Phalange party – could
very easily replace the social functions undertaken by a modern state.
In fact, so long as the Maronites have recourse to their zaim, their
family, their emigrés, their party, and their community, they could not
care less about the expansion of the functions of the state.

No mention is ever made about partition in Maronite official statements.   But this is not indicative of the strength of the partitionists.
Against this, the greatest asset of the integrationists is the strong opposition of Lebanon's neighbours and of all major foreign powers to the idea
of partition.   But although their aim is totally unrealistic – taking into
consideration the international scene – the partitionists can muster
considerable support from the rank and file of the parties and militias;
and they have managed to maintain a controlled tension by creating
everyday incidents aimed at establishing a political climate favourable
to partition.   When the Pope's envoy, Bertoli, arrived in Beirut, he
thought that the close links Rome had with the Maronites would make it
easier for him to convince the latter to make concessions in order to
safeguard their experience of communal co-existence.   But he soon had
to realise that the traditional leaders were prisoners of the 'street,'
of the new military zaims – those whom a journalist described as 'the
unripe (fajjah) leaders propelled onto the political scene by the barri-
cades.'   For their part, many Maronites thought that Bertoli had come
to 'sell out' the Christians, that he was not the Pope's envoy but the
envoy of an Italy which had a communist majority, that 'the smell of
oil was now overtaking the incense in the churches of Europe and
America.'[9]

Backed by the foreign powers, the moderates within the Maronite
community have recently (late 1975) benefitted from the change in Prime
Minister Karami's attitude (tikawee'a) and the anti-leftist campaign

led by the traditional Moslem leadership.   In other words, the Moslem
section of the ruling group was making overtures to its Maronite counter-
part in order to recreate the old alliance, it being understood that each
party would have to clean up its own 'street'.   This was followed by
conciliatory statements on behalf of Franjeih and Gemayel who absolved
the Moslems and put the blame for the fighting on subversive elements.
Meanwhile, in December 1975, Assem Qanso, the pro-Syrian Ba'thist
leader made a statement clearing Pierre Gemayel and blaming   the
'isolationists' (in 'izaliyyun).   A few days later, Gemayel went to
Damascus.   But the truce between Karami and Gemayel threatens the
truce between Karami and Jumblat.   Moreover, the rapprochement
which is taking place between the Maronites and the Syrians (December
1975) frightens the Palestinians.   Finally it has become clear that the
traditional Moslem leaders are not in control of the situation.   Their
position has been undermined by the gains which the Left has made within the Moslem ranks beginning even before the fighting broke out, by
the strength of the extremist Maronites which has paralyzed the moderates, and, ironically, by the attitude of Franjieh since he came to power.
We can all recall that when the Lebanese army and the Palestinians
fought each other in 1973, Franjieh refused to allow the Moslem leadership to mediate between the Palestinians and the Christians, wanting to
deal with them both directly himself; this cannot have helped the
position of the Moslem leaders vis à vis their 'street' or the Palestinians.

To look to the future, if the Moslem ruling groups do not manage to
dissociate themselves from the Left without losing their power and
influence, the Maronite ruling groups will have increasing difficulty in
controlling the partitionists.[10]   Partition is not only opposed by all
foreign countries but also by the Christian and Moslem economic elites
and entrepreneurs because of its anti-capitalist character.   Both the
Christian 'Petit Liban' and the left-wing, radical state which may border
it would not be a paradise for private enterprise.   Without discussing
a problematic Lebano-Palestinian radical state, we can still speculate
about the future of a right-wing Christian state.   For one thing, such a
state would need a great amount of foreign financial assistance, mainly
from the Maronite diaspora overseas.   But to keep the money flowing
in the name of Maronite solidarity, the Maronite state must maintain a
minimum cohesion within its borders.   Moreover, the leaders of this
Maronite state would not be able to act in the same way in which the
Israeli leaders are acting, ie by entertaining a climate of tension on the
borders and by emphasising the importance of the common enemy in
order to overcome internal contradictions.   They could not do this

because the 'Petit Liban' would still need the Arab hinterland, the
emigrés money constituting only a temporary expedient.   Hence the only
way of maintaining the cohesion of the Maronite community (i e the sole
justification for a Maronite state) would be to establish an egalitarian,
corporatist state – a kind of national-socialist state.

Of course, before we reach such an extreme, we must not rule out
an intervention by supra-party army officers, backed by the simple wish
to live normally.   Such an intervention would have to accompany its
repressive character – falling equally on the extreme Left and the extreme
Right – by an impulse towards drastic reforms and a clear programme
aimed at the expansion of the role of the state, and thus the increasing
homogenization of society. [11]

But if the army should prove too divided to intervene, the best
solution seems to lie in the creation of a federal state with complete
administrative and political decentralisation: the minimum programme
of the partitionists.   The prospect of an independent and autonomous
Maronite state depends on the ability of the emerging leadership (be it
composed of new men or of the traditional leaders who have managed to
shift priorities and to put communal interests above economic considerations) to hold on militarily and to support the Maronite traditions of the
common people. *   But, most important of all, the future of a Maronite
state must certainly lie in the ability of the leaders to enlist the support
of a major foreign power.   Every new day of bitter fighting, of sectarian murders and of economic destruction increases the possibility of
partition.   And even if the international context does not allow for the
establishment of a Maronite state, the Maronites themselves are showing clearly that, following the Pan-Syrians and the Pan-Arabs, they too
reject the choice of a Grand Liban. [12]

All through the Lebanese crisis one can pinpoint errors of judgement
made by the various politicians and political parties, errors which may
be seen as so many turning points leading to a further escalation of

---

* It is interesting to look at the names of the militias such as the
  Defenders of the Cedars, the Phalange of Fear, the Marada, the Wood
  of the Cross, the Youth of St Marun, and the Knights of the Virgin.
  In this respect the leadership has been helped greatly by the strong
  attachment of the young people to values, symbols and objects which
  would seem obsolete by European standards: the prestige of uniform,
  martial tradition, the status attached to possession of a weapon, the
  emphasis placed on courage, temerity, strength, machismo, etc.

violence: Ma'ruf Sa'ad's coffin wrapped in the Palestinian flag, the
Christian demonstration in support of the army, the inability of the Phalange to evaluate the true nature of the political gains made by the Left
at Saida, the Left's demand for the political isolation of the Phalange,
the inability of the Left to realise that its alliance with the Palestinian
movement was not as 'natural' as it seemed, and the way in which the
Moslem elite's choice of the game of modernity and rationality left them
captives of the illusion of a liberal, Westernised Lebanon.   But most
important of all was the original error made in 1920.   This was for the
elites to make their decision as to the future relations of the various
communities on the basis of economic and geopolitical (or, at the international level, ideological) considerations, all of which were practically
irrelevent as far as the common people were concerned.   From   a
Maronite point of view such a choice could only be justified as long as
they could regard Lebanon as being their's.   The present crisis is an
indication of the disillusion of the Maronites, leading to their rejection
of the choice made on their behalf in 1920.   It is the revenge of the
'small' Maronite, the hick, the red-neck, over the typical figure of the
entrepreneur who has been caught and tied up by the Discourse he was
holding.

But beyond the errors made by the parties, we should include the
responsibility of all intellectuals and students of Lebanese society,
whether Lebanese or foreign, who now have to bear their share of responsibility for what is happening.   Right-wingers, we were eager to
praise the Lebanese experience of democracy and liberalism, to compare
it with the West, and to set it up as an example for other developing
countries;   left-wingers, we have situated our struggle on the grounds
offered by the Right, the French Mandate, international politics and the
requirements for world stability.   Being true products of an advanced
society, we, leftists as much as rightists, have not been able to understand that the 'Mask' of confessionalism which we were either using or
condemning - according to one's political beliefs - was not a mask after
all, or rather that it was only a mask in our own westernized minds.*
The present crisis is proof enough that the Illusion did not lie in

---

* Confessionalism is, of course, only one among many other aspects of
  the segmentation of the Lebanese society.   Analysing, for example,
  the Maronite sect, one should push one's analysis well beyond the
  apparent unity of the community - even in times of crisis - and examine
  more basic units of internal differentiation: family, village, clan,

confessionalism but rather in the fallacy of the liberal and westernized state, and in the absence of homogeneous social classes, let alone class consciousness and class solidarity.

References:

1   I F Harik, Politics and Change in a Traditional Society: Lebanon
     1711-1854 (Princeton, 1968), p128
2   M Rodinson, Marxisme et Monde Musulman (Paris, 1972), p667.
3   L Z Yamak, The Syrian Social Nationalist Party: An Ideological
     Analysis (Cambridge, 1966), p36
4   J Entelis, Pluralism and Party Transformation in Lebanon :
     Al-Kata'ib 1936-1970 (Leiden, 1974)
5   Antoine, Najm, interviewed by Entelis in Beirut, 11 March 1969,
     Entelis, p71
6   Entelis, p160
7   'Mudhakkira marfu'a 'ila fathamat ra'is al-jumhuriyya al-'ustadh
     Sulayman Faranjiyya', Phalange Party mimeo, Beirut, 19 Feb
     1973, p9 in F Stoakes, 'The supervigilantes .....', Middle Eastern
     Studies, X, 3 (Oct 1975), p222
8   Salim Nasser, 'Muhimmat al-Vatican tukammiluha Paris',
     Al-Hawardith, 993, 21 Nov 1975.
9   'I'adat tarkib al-watam al-lubnani', Al-Hawardith, 993, 21 Nov
     1975.
10   This paper was written in November 1975, long before the Syrian
     intervention. It may be said that Syria aims at playing the role

region. It is quite obvious, for example, that the Northern Maronites are very different from the Southerners. The unequal impact of the Phalange Party on the various Maronite areas posits the same kind of question. The Phalange appears to have done well in backward regions (the different Jurds) while it was unable to supplant the traditional notables in the more prosperous areas of the Sahel. The one backward region where the Party had little success is the North (Zghorta, Bisharri), where the family structure is very strong. In all prosperous regions where the Party has done well (eg Metn) it has done so through the transformation of the notables (Gemayel) into Party workers, and it has succeeded because in such regions the Party and its organization were necessary to counter the influence of other parties (eg PPS, CP).

which the traditional Moslem leadership can no longer play, ie to
get the Moslems under control;   this being the sine qua non condition for a resumption of the traditional inter-community consensus.
But an eventual consensus of that sort would have to be implemented
through the main political parties and armed organizations, and
not, as in 1943, through the traditional notables.   Syria is well
aware that the Moslem notables have been supplanted by the Left
and the PLO, and that is why President Assad is gambling on the
Phalange, knowing that only a party at this level of organization
and mobilization could match the Leftist parties and the PLO, and
offer to the Maronites the degree of security necessary for a
minimum amount of trust to be restored.   Syria is offering the
Phalange a way out of the dangerous impasse they were drawn in
since April 1975.   The new consensus would engage the Phalange
Party on the one hand, the Leftist parties and the PLO 'guaranteed'
by Syria on the other hand, with Elias Sarkis, a person without
traditional root support being highly dependent on Syria and playing
the role of the supra-community President.

11   The army did prove too divided to intervene.   Its role was thus
taken over by the Syrian-backed troops.

12   The constant use, throughout this paper, of the terms 'Maronites'
and 'Maronite community' is only for purpose of simplification.
Beyond these monolythical terms we are dealing with the persons,
groups and parties who, in specific historical circumstances,
successfully manage to pose as the true representatives of the
material, cultural and spiritual interests of those Lebanese who
adhere to the ideology of 'Maronitism'.

THE PROGRESSIVE FORCES

by Aziz Al-Azmeh

Whereas the Phalange and other rightist forces engaged in the present
civil war in the Lebanon claim in their literature that they, as the true
guardians of the Fatherland, are waging a war of defence against a con-
spiracy hatched by foreigners and international communism, the prime
target of the Left is the forces of Lebanese isolationism.   The conscious target of the Right is very telling. The name it has given its
enemies is typical of a universal tendency among the spokesmen of ruling
elites by which internal disorder is automatically attributed to the play
of elements not proper to the regime itself.   No system admits that it
has been superseded, and the Right, in arrogating to itself the role of
the political elite and guardianship of the system, stakes a claim to
represent what technocratic notions lead it to call a 'modern state'.
Within such a perspective, the Right professes to be fighting the
enemies of the regime in the shape of a horde of unaccountable origin.
Against this the Left does not think it is waging a war against the power
of a modern state as much as against an archaic and ottomanesque group
of forces, be they the Phalange, the Guardians of the Cedar or St Marun's
Bretheren in Islam.   For the Left, the rightist coalition is a group of
backward, clannish forces which have usurped the wealth of the nation to
the benefit of their atavistic exclusivity.   They are considered as forces

---

This essay was written in March 1976.

which base their control of the economic and political fortunes of the state upon pillars that emanate from and reinforce a feudal politics.

The name given to the Right, the 'Isolationists,' not only implies that these forces seek to isolate Lebanon from Arab patriotic tendencies but also connotes, more importantly, sectarian exclusivity within the country and thus evokes political support that springs from opposition to both politico-confessional and class exclusivity.   Isolationism being thus a potent indicator that points to more than one strand along which political and civil forces can operate, it also indicates the diversity of the forces which can operate under the leftist coalition.   They are by no means reducible to uniform political, social, economic, or ideological structures, nor is it easy to delineate or trace them within the Lebanese context, where the situation presents itself as juxtaposition of forces that are the products of very uneven social, economic, and regional developments.[1]   A search for the element that not so much subsumes the others as much as imposes a measure of operational unity upon them, will reveal that the present situation is one which is overdetermined by the political instance.   It is one in which the Left is a conjunctural set of heterogeneous forces operationally homogenised at the level of politics, which is itself a product of the breakdown of the civil hegemonies of the old order and of the tenuous ideological project of the state.

Some conditions of this heterogeneity can be elucidated from an examination of the position occupied by Lebanon's capital, Beirut. The country was in fact constructed around its capital.   Lebanon being a geopolitical entity demarcated as a result of factors external to the inner constitution of the territory, its development followed the exigencies of the power structure formed at its centre.   Beirut was the point of geographical concentration of population and of non-agricultural activities, basically in trade, while the diffusion[2] of these activities and of the benefits accruing from them obeyed imperatives that were political and not economic. Political influence and not the demands of market 'rationality' determined the economic diffusion of Beirut into areas whose prosperity it underpinned, while those areas, such as the South and the North, whose communitarian elites had no such access to the spoils of office, were penetrated by the logic of the Beirut market in such a way that they became a dumping ground for imported wares in exchange for which they had scarcely anything to offer.   The result of this was that there was no penetration of the political structures of the Lebanese geopolitical entity by the new economic imperatives based upon the capitalist relations that obtained within the services mode of production on which rested the prosperity of the bourgeoisie of the politically favoured areas, and which also formed

the base for political feudalism – a product not only of the services
mode of production but also of the system of economic and civil rewards
for political service.   With the simultaneous persistence of the titular
mode of production,[3] ie of service either to the landlord or to the tobacco
monopoly, a system of regional economic dislocations was consolidated
which confirmed the politico-regional structures of domination and confined economic interest groups to a very rudimentary corporate organisation.

In view of this, it would be instructive to examine some of the areas
where the civil war is being waged.   In the central and western Biqaa
the struggle is one primarily between the town of Zahle, a trading centre
favoured because of the accessibility of economic benefits from Beirut
to its patricians and passed down the social ladder to their political
clients, and the surrounding countryside where the forces of the Communist Party (CP) and Organisation of Communist Action in Lebanon (OCAL)
and the Baath are active.   The peasantry has been reduced to a prolet-
ariat by the capitalist investment in agriculture and in the light industries
set up in the region.   The intellectuals in the area suffer from the lack
of possibilities for promotion because they have no access to the patronage system based in Zahle.   In addition to these forces supporting the
left, the PLO and the Army of Arab Lebanon (AAL) played an important
role in securing the military isolation of the town because of its strategic importance, which it owes to its geographical location dominating
a main road junction linking the Biqaa with Syria and Beirut, and the
North of the valley with the South.

The north-west presents a different picture.   There the struggle is
both between what the media call 'rival Christian factions' and also
between Zghorta and Tripoli.   The 'rival factions' are the Syrian
Social Nationalist Party (SSNP) forces of the Kura, south of Zghorta,
and the Zghorta Liberation Army, a clannish formation.   This clash is
both economic and ideological, just like the one between Zghorta and
Tripoli.   For Zghorta, especially since President Frangieh came to
power, has been expanding and trying to assume the role of economic
centre in the north, so that natives of Zghorta were even trying to assume positions of economic dominance in Tripoli itself.   As for
Tripoli the main forces are the Iraq Baath, the CP the OCAL and 24th
Of October movement.   The participation of the AAL secured the isolation of Zghorta.

In Mount Lebanon the battle has been, militarily, one for securing
control over vital strategic roads.   Here the left-wing offensive was
mounted under the auspices of the United Forces, the military

coordination committee of the left-wing military organizations, and the
main participants were Jumblat's Druze forces, the AAL, the OCAL,
in addition to local forces of the SSNP and the CP.   Finally in Beirut the
left is represented by the militarily very important Independent Nasserists (IN) and their militia, the Murabitun, who have a wide Arabist and
populist appeal, along with similar forces and the politically very important CP and OCAL which control and administer the large suburbs such as
Shiyyah, inhabited by Shi^{c}i immigrants from the south and the Biqaa.
The Shi^{c}a in effect experienced a political birth. Coming from very
poor and backward areas, driven to Beirut by systematic Israeli attempts
to depopulate the South and by the constant deterioration of their economic
condition, they congregated in over-crowded agglomerations on the peri-
phery of Beirut and entered into the industrial sector as wage labourers.
The Shi^{c}a bourgeoisie being of very recent formation and involved in a
subaltern function for the ruling elite both economically and politically,
the labouring masses were left to their own devices deprived of the
traditional protection afforded by the structures of civil society which are
the pillar of the Lebanese political formation. Those Shi^{c}is inhabiting
the 'miserty belt' of suburbs surrounding Beirut came to see the city as
a true 'bastard offspring of Cain', as it was called by the dialect poet
Karim al-Karki.   Their civil and political dislocation from the structures
of the regime is complete.   Attempts to set up sectarian Shi^{c}i organizations were very short lived.   The 'Movement of the Disinherited' of the
Imam Musa as-Sadr, as well as his military organization, Fityan Ali,
had hardly got beyond a few mass rallies when the Shi^{c}is decided they
did not want to star in a bad melodrama and opted for the leadership of men like George Hawi of the CP, a Greek Orthodox from the Matn,
or Fawwaz Trabulsi, of the OCAL, a Catholic from the southern Biqaa.

The dislocation of political structures based upon civic leadership
is not only confined to the Shi^{c}a but is also part of a process that affected all sectarian and regional communities, the only exception being the
Maronites, whose leaders' accessibility to the spoils of office acted
to reinforce the civil structure of their politics based on parochial considerations.   In Beirut and Tripoli analogous situations led to the
emergence of organizations such as the 24th of October movement and
the IN, which recruited their members from among the groups that had
previously provided the political clientele of traditional leaders such as
Saeb Salam and Rashid Karami.

Such a transference of the field of social relations upon which traditional Sunni leaders based their power to agents of political activity from
a different provenance was the result of a configuration of different

factors, and signified dislocation in the lineage-structured sphere of civil society. It also meant the direct transposition of social and economic struggles to the political sphere, ie to the sphere of state power and of those forces whose conflict takes place within the confines of the space described by the logic of direct accessibility to state power. The reason for this was that the wall of opacity and mystification surrounding the regime and constructed out of the community-based institutions of civil society was bored through at its very foundations by the policy of Shehabism and fell with its demise. Shehabism had tried to institute checks upon the operations of civil relations in order to make the state the sole political unit in the country. Its Deuxième Bureau was supposed to displace the traditional chieftains by taking over their role as the sole za^{c}im from whom state benefits would be obtained. In pursuit of this policy the Deuxième Bureau promoted the rise in the Sunni areas of more or less popular leaderships who capitalised on their role in the 1958 civil war and who were outside the control of traditional leaders. It was this organisation that provided Ibrahim Kuleilat with the means and the avenues that were eventually used to build up a working power base. In the late sixties, the Deuxième Bureau also promoted the Imam Sadr as an antidote to the influence of Kamil al-As^{c}d in the South. Such new leaders largely functioned with traditional methods as vehicles of patronage, but they had partly displaced the urban patricians in their functions as patricians. With the dismantling of the Shihabist Deuxième Bureau in the wake of Franjieh's accession to the Presidency, these organizations lost their role as components in the wall of opacity which slurred the real nature of political issues by transforming them into civil technicalities such as the arithmetic of confessional balance in the Civil Service. Instead they became mere popular organizations, sustaining themselves by the sheer momentum they had previously acquired.

Separate factors of two distinct orders then converged to form a political conjuncture that propelled these organisations forward. Economically, the vast influx of oil money into Lebanon was partly responsible for leaping inflation which led to an increasing destitution of the middle classes revealing that the 'Lebanese miracle' was to the benefit of only a small and ostentatious minority, the so-called 'four percent'. This in turn increased the corruption of the already corrupt to such an extent that the Civil Service could not even provide the bare minimum of public services, such as water and electricity. Meanwhile, the traditional leaderships failed to fulfil even their most elementary communitarian duties, and whatever influence that remained was finally eroded.

The more important factor was ideological. The pan-Arab radical-
izing effects of the 1976 war was complemented and concretised by the
presence in Lebanon of the Palestinian resistance. Just after the war
the Arab Nationalist Movement (ANM) adopted a platform that included
the adoption of Marxism as a doctrinal principle, thus completing a
trend that had started a couple of years previously. In addition to this
organisational marxism, a strong trend toward marxism among Arab
intellectuals had Lebanon as its vortex. The late sixties and early
seventies saw the appearance of numerous books, pamphlets, and period-
icals that were highly influential among intellectuals and students.
Publication in Beirut was booming, and readership multiplied several
fold. The clandestine review Lubnan al-Ishtiraki produced marxist
analyses of the economic and political structures in Lebanon that remain
the best products of Arab marxism. Ideological radicalisation also
reached the fringes of the ecclesiastical establishment with the creation
in 1974 of the Mouvement Social of Mgr Gregoire Haddad, the Greek
Catholic bishop of Beirut, and of its journal Afaq. The bishop was subsequently removed from office for taking a politically anti-clerical
line   on humanistic grounds and for attacking the establishment and
the status quo in no uncertain terms. Later, during the present civil
war, Mgr Haddad formed 'consciousness raising' committees to prepare for a secular Lebanon. His appeal was strong among young intellectuals - the sons and daughters of the establishment affiliated to the
CP and OCAL and among students, many of whom subsequently joined
one of these two organizations, some to be killed in action during the
civil war.

The period after the 1967 war was also one of intensive attempts to
forge links between the various marxist organisations founded by
intellectuals - the most prominent of whom were the scions of more or
less well-to-do families from the Shi^{ci} South   and the trades unions.
Such attempts were not always successful, but inroads into corporate
organizations of workers were made easier after a split, never formal-
ized, between the shop-floor representatives and the leadership early
in 1974. A significant fact in this context is that most of the workers
thus organized came from the South. And it is also very significant
that, during Jumblat's tenure of the Ministry of the Interior in 1970
and 1971, in which the SSNP and the CP were legalised, young men's
clubs proliferated in the villages of the South under the auspices of the
Shi^{ci} schools, al-husayniyat, and formed centres for the acquisition
and dissemination of political culture organised by radical groups.

However, the most potent factor which, at the popular level,

precipitated the collapse of the political rampart built of the structures
given to the Lebanese geopolitical entity at its inception - the mediation
of informal civil institutions - was the advent of the Palestinians upon the
scene as a vividly visible symbol around which political positions aligned
themselves, thereby absorbing economic and ideological parameters
within the political. Through the Palestinians, the Lebanese entity was
reinserted into its Arab context and deprived of that artifical isolation
which had hitherto served to maintain the political safeguards necessary
for its international economic role.   Inside Lebanon Nasserism had been
the ideological analogue of the type of Arab nationalism supported by the
ANM in Palestinian and other Arab circles.   However, while the ANM
turned towards marxism, Lebanese Nasserism did not and the movement
continued to function as a civil group rather than as a political party
and to incorporate an archaic conception establishing a vague association
between Arabism and Islam - for the latter was intrinsically
associated with the communitarian principles according to which it opera-
ted.   The other connotative component of Lebanese Nasserism, its
populism, was reinforced by the demise of Shehabism. The advent of
the Palestinians and the clumsiness with which the Sunni traditional
leaders dealt with them effected a condensation of the two above ideological components within a space described and bounded by the only
means open within the Lebanese political context of effectively defending
the Palestinian presence in the country: 'true nationalism' as the
rejection of the status quo. Political radicalism, the bypassing of
civil buffers surrounding the state, thus became the prime component
in the memory of Arab nationalism. And along with the displacement
of the traditional Sunni leadership in its capacity as Muslim leadership
came an ideological displacement of the islamic component of nationalism whose nationalist functions were taken over by political radicalism.
The entire web of normative ascription attaching to nationalism was
transferred wholesale to the Palestinians and to the political issues that
were raised as a consequence of their presence in the country.
     The use of traditional civic avenues for building popular Nasserist
organizations did not impair the power of this ideological assault on the
institutions of the state.   For one thing, the proper functioning of
civil relations implied the leaders' accessibility to the spoils of power,
and this was no longer the case for Nasserist leaders after the political
folklore of the Maronite establishment and other elements within the
traditional leadership had defeated the project of the Deuxieme Bureau.
The power of patronage was so reduced that the cushioning effect played
by communitarianism was no longer possible.   Thus the only mode of

action left was the political;   ideas that had been in termination
began their transmutation into political parties.

The situation called for some programmatic thinking, since politics
as manoeuvre à la libanaise was no longer possible.   Thus ideology contained the quintessential condensation of economic, social and political
situations, while the political conjuncture overdetermined an ideological
moment which made for their effective political coherence, their unity
as a party to a struggle that took the form of armed conflict and thus im-
pinged back onto the components and transposed them into politics, for
war is a purified extension of politics.   The wall of opacity was thus
penetrated, and the political system was no longer cushioned by civil
institutions.   Politics became a game played properly within the context
of the real balance of power which, in Lebanon, meant the dismantling of
the confessional system whose result was daily seen as dessicated and
powerless parliamentarism.   This gave rise to the call for proportional
representation in parliament a major demand of the Left-wing coalition
during the present civil war, as a way of replacing the pawn-shop parliament of today.*

All these developments occurred in the context of the intense popular
and intellectual turmoil that marked the period which began on April 12
1969, when the security forces dispersed a demonstration of protest
against Lebanese army activities directed against the Palestinians and
shot dead a considerable number of demonstrators.   The result was a
prolonged crisis of the regime, with martial law and seven months without a government.

Yet it should be noted that not all of the largely Sunni organizations
took this leftward secular and radical trend.   Some continued to operate
on strictly confessional and civil lines, such as the private militia of
Faruk Shihab-ad-Din in the Basta quarters of Beirut, and the Islamic
Association (at-tajammu al-islami) of Tripoli which is sympathetic with
the Muslim Brothers.   Yet such movements remained marginal and
usually confined to sections of quarters, for the Islamic community they
were trying to revive no longer had, as the Maronites did, communitarian
superstructures of civil society bounded by the ideology of Lebanism
that could act as trenches in a war of positions.   Such residues of
traditional confessionalism are unimportant in any effective sense today

---

* This tendency was spelled out long before the civil war when Najah
  Wakim, a Greek Orthodox, was elected a member of Parliament in
  a Sunni area of Beirut on the basis of a populist and Nasserist
  platform.

yet such movements have participated, emotionally and, in some cases, militarily, with the Left-wing forces which are grouped around what has been termed the cause of the Palestinians.   Their participation was not political.   Nevertheless their presence serves to underline the fact that the forces which now constitute the Left have been grouped around what we may call a minimum programme symbolized by support for the Palestinians in Lebanon and elsewhere.   This programme, as has been intimated, served as a sign of a definite ideological orientation   with broad if unmistakable political connotations.   Moreover, due to the variety of factors we have been considering that were conducive to the rise of the Left, it can be seen that the range of associations and meanings implied by this sign is vast, thus making it accessible to groups of various natures and origins and transforming it into a principle of cohesion.

Nevertheless it is difficult to believe that this principle of cohesion is solely internal to the constitution of the left.   To a large extent it depends on the enemy and on the metamorphoses it has gone through before and during the civil war.   The political unity is thus, to a large extent, polemical in that it depends as much on the enemy as it does on its protagonists.   <u>Support for the Palestinians is not merely a point of orientation, it is also a criterion of exclusion</u>.   In other words, the issue of support for the Palestinians has acted as a factor unifying those groups which, for various reasons, adopted such support as an immediate political aim, thus excluding from the political pale all forces that either opposed the Palestinians or else wavered on this point.   It is a criterion of ideological inclusion in that it has served to <u>assimilate</u> nationalistic political instincts, such as those of the IN or of the AAL into the ideological radicalism of the groups that had been constituted originally as <u>political parties,</u> transforming what are professedly 'purely military' formations into part of a political campaign whose mode of action had become military.   This political homogenisation is well expressed in the political slogan that accompanied the leftist offensive in March 1976. The war is a 'war of unification', a march towards the 'new unified, democratic, and secular Lebanon'.[4] The confessional instincts unleashed by the rightist forces in the first few months of the civil war had been politically superseded on the Left, and what had been a motley of isolated and uncoordinated forces fighting the Right witnessed a definite move towards unification throughout the latter part of 1975 (see the Appendix below).

In fact, the past few years, especially since 1969, have witnessed several attempts to make, unmake, and remake coalitions of left-wing and national forces, grouped around the issue of support for the Pales-

tinian resistance against the hostility of the regime and of the Right. None
of these were really effective, and collapsed as a result of the lack of
any real principle of homogeneity beyond a vague adherence to the notion
of the sanctity of the Palestinians which, as has been shown, spring from
many causes.   At this stage the Resistance had to rely on its own resources, and surrounded itself by individual Lebanese who owed allegiance
to no particular local forces but who were dedicated to its cause.   The
civil war then created the conjuncture which, by giving primacy to the
political, made the effective forging of a radicalising unity possible.
This happened not only because the nationalist support for the Palestinians was now inseparable from an association with internal social and
political issues, but also because the behaviour and pronouncements of
the rightist forces accelerated the process and made it into a day-to-day
reality.   In this way a vague Pro-Palestinianism began to be translated
into concrete political demands.   A vital factor in this transformation
was the changes in the nature of political contention as the civil war pro-
gressed.   It started off as an attempt to defend the Palestinian resistance in the face of attack by both the Right and the State.   At this stage
the forces were still very heterogeneous, and the unity instinctive.   The
war then took on clear confessional connotations with the extension of
both the rightist offensive and of the national forces drawn to battle.
But this extension of the conflict created a military and ideological necessity for coordination on the part of the Left and national forces,
leading to a process of unification of the Nasserist forces around a single
pole of attraction, the IN.   This process in turn necessitated the dissolution of parochial groupings within a wider movement, something which
resulted naturally in involvement in issues that went far beyond even
parochial considerations as the fighting of individual units administration of small groups based on such factors as locality and
lineage.   The civil level of necessity superseded, and the winter of
1975/76 witnessed the dissolution of heterogeneity within the crucible
of politics extended into war as the only effective means of political
action.

    Simultaneous with this change was the contraction of the enemy and
its confinement to the Maronite Right after the State had ceased to exist
and while the army was disintegrating. Significantly, in March 1976,
the Maronite monks decided that the solution to the crisis should take the
form, not of explicit confessional representation, nor of proportional
representation, but of representation on the basis of 'quality'.[5] This not
only led Jumblat to compare Lebanon with Rhodesia when talking to
foreign journalists, it also underscored the Maronite leadership's

awareness of the fact that a re-allocation of political spoils on the basis of confessional proportions would mean that, in the long run, the Maronites are in for a period in which their position and privileges will be gradually eroded as a prelude to their transformation into a mere confessional minority which has no rights but those of a minority .

This insistence of the Maronite leadership on its confessional character and the privileges that were confirmed by it led to the expansion of the Left militarily and to a concretisation of its political demands in the form of a reformist programme which, though mild by general standards, is revolutionary in Lebanese terms, for it envisages the total scrapping of the old political order.   Furthermore, this brought it in touch with personalities who were by no means revolutionaries, such as Raymond Edde, a Maronite who had already undergone political circumcision as aspirant to the Presidency in the election won by Sarkis, and who was also supported by traditional Sunni leaderships or like Brigadier Aziz al-Ahdab, author of the platonic military coup of March 1976.

It was this insistence on Maronite confessionalism that led to the leftist offensive which drove the rightists out of the Beirut port area and which contested their control over the harbour, as well as to the war in Mount Lebanon, their geographical base and the heartland of their political fief.   In the latter, the left-wing forces wrested control over road junctions in a campaign designed to pressure the Right into acknowledg-- ing the realities of the balance of political forces within the country. It was not aimed at occupation, however, and military operations took the form of small raids as well as of arranging generous surrender terms for villages previously controlled by the rightist forces, such as Ain Dara, in which only heavy arms were confiscated - just as had previously happened when the Shuf was neutralised in the wake of the Karantina massacre and the capture of Damur.

These developments brought the rightist leadership face to face with a harsh choice.   Either they could declare an autonomous state, with all the economic and political problems this would entail: it would be unprofitable and would fail to include an estimated 75 percent of the Christian, and 50 percent of the Maronite population which lived in the rest of the country over which they had no control.   Or, alternatively, they would have had to forfeit leadership in their capacity as Maronites.

Such was the situation that witnessed external military and political intervention in the country, starting effectively in January 1976.   With Syrian military pressure and international and Arab attempts to bring in peace-keeping forces - each proposition at odds with the others - the archaic leadership of the Right was saved from making this decision.

An ad hoc arrangement is under way with the appointment of Sarkis to
the Presidency.   Unlike the long-term outcome of conflicts, its immediate results do not lend themselves to divination.   The extent of ethical-
ideological hegemony that the Left has managed to accumulate is immense,
but it is impossible to gauge the extent to which it can be officialised
so long as the Left lacks political power and given its possible political
fragmentation.   What renders immediate possibilities even more in-
tractable is the configuration of regional and international forces that
are leading towards attempts at transforming Lebanon into an international protectorate and to the impositions of a neo-Shehabism.   In view of
these attempts to waylay history by making it repetitive,it would be
well to invert Marx's dictum and say that when history repeats itself,
the first spectacle is a farce and the second time over, a disaster.[6]

Appendix: Components of the left-wing and national movement.

Marxist Organizations

The main Marxist organizations are the Communist Party (CP) and the
Organization for Communist Action in Lebanon (OCAL), and there has
always been a transient population of tiny Maoist and Trotskyist groups
which merged into the two main parties or splintered off from them.
The CP has a long-established power base in the unions, in Tripoli,
and in the Matn village of Btighrin.   The OCAL was formed in 1970 as
the result of the merger of the Lebanese branch of the ANM with the
group formed around the review Lubnan al-ishtiraki.   There was bitter
organisational rivalry and differences between the two groups at the out-
set, but the civil war brought them into close cooperation, and the OCAL
has grown considerably during the war, supplanting the influence of
Imam Sadr both in the South and in the suburbs of Beirut.
In close alliance with these main forces is the left-wing Marxist faction
of the Kurdish Democratic Party which was affiliated to the Front of
Progressive and National Forces in 1973.   There also exists the Arab
Socialist Action Party, formed of the remainder of the ANM in 1969,
and closely allied with George Habash.

Radical Organizations

Except for Tripoli and Akkar, the two Baath parties are occasional
organizations which provide material means for the functioning of other
groups; during the civil war, the Syrian Baath was allied with Imam Sadr
and the Shatila faction of the Union of the Forces of the Working People
(UFWP - see below), as well as with the Jamil Da'bul faction of the
Najjada Party in Shiyyah, before the suburb was controlled by the CP and
the OCAL.

Kamal Jumblat's Progressive People's Party consists mainly of intellectuals and students, and its main military muscle comes from Jumblat's
clansmen in the Shuf. The Syrian Social Nationalist Party (SSNP) has
gone through a period of frequent splits and secessions in the past few
years, but has consistently taken a pro-Palestinian and anti-Phalangist
line, as well as having a radical secularist programme. It has important concentrations in the Matn and Kura. It has now changed its name
to the National Social Party.

Nationalists and Radical Nationalists

There is a confusing profusion of such organizations, often confined to
one locality. The main components are the Independent Nasserists of
Ibrahim Kuleilat and the Shatila faction of the UFWP in Beirut, the 14th
October Movement of Faruk al-Muqaddim in Tripoli, and Popular
Nasserist Organization in Sidon led by 'Admiral Nelson' Mustafa Ma'ruf
Sa'd, so called after he had shelled Jiyyeh from fishing boats. There
now exists an alliance between Kuleilat, Muqaddim, Sa'd, the Army of Arab
Lebanon, and the Marxist and radical left when, late in 1975, Kuleilat
brought together the disparate Nasserist forces in Beirut and welded them
into an effective fighting force, compelling the smaller factions either to
come under his leadership or to contract within their localities. Some
survived under Baathist auspices, such as the Shatila faction based in
the Beirut districts of Aisha Bakkar and Burj Abu Haidar, and other
organizations of small-time political racketeering.
The Army of Arab Lebanon falls within this group.

Local and Sectarian Organizations

There are several such groups which carry out local defence and racketeering work, sometimes on behalf of traditional leaders. Musa Sadr's
Fityān Ali is one such group that still has some influence in the Nabaa
suburb. The Basta quarter of Beirut is dominated by the Supporters of
the Revolution, a group that leans towards the Muslim Brothers. It is
sponsored by Al Fatah and has clashed with the Saiqa on several
occasions. Some power is also exercised in the Basta by Faruk Shihab

ad-Din's Democratic Reform Front, consisting of a handful of thugs in
the pay of Saeb Salam.   A former thug of Salam's, Hassan Ido, is active
in the Bashura quarter where he controls the protection racket over the
cemeteries.   It is also thought that Salam is sponsoring the Eagles of
Zaidaniya which, through the Itani family, is trying to control the quarter.
Several other similar organizations exist which are even more insignifi
cant than the ones mentioned.

Footnotes

1   For an analysis of the background of the civil war, see the very
     important article of W Sharara, 'Rabī^C 1975 al-Lubnanī', in Dirāsāt
     Arabīya, vol XI, no 12, October 1975, pp9-42.
2   For developments of this notion, see J. Friedman et al 'Urbanisation
     et developpement national', in Tiers-Monde, XII (1971), pp 14-19
3   S Amin, Le developpement inégal, Paris 1973, ch I
4   al-Hurrīya, 29.3.1976, pp I, 8
5   al-Hawādith, 15.3.1976, p 10
6   See E Rouleau in Le Monde, 1, 2, 3, 4 June, 1976

THE PALESTINIAN ARMED PRESENCE IN LEBANON SINCE 1967

by Hussein Sirriyyeh

This paper discusses the impact of the Palestinian armed presence in the
Lebanon on Lebanese politics since the June war of 1967, along with the
role played by the Lebanese political setting in conditioning this impact.
This central theme is dealt with by presenting an overview of the development of the Palestinian armed presence in the Lebanon since 1967,
focusing on the Palestinian roles in, and attitudes towards, the present
civil war in the Lebanon, and then by appraising the general impact of the
Palestinian armed presence on Lebanese politics. While the paper con-
centrates mainly on the above theme, an attempt is made to view the
Palestinian armed presence in the Lebanon through the larger context of
Palestinian-Arab relations. This is done by presenting a brief sketch
of the post-June 1967 factors connected with the re-emergence of the
Palestinian armed resistance and then by examining the impact of this
resistance on the politics of the host Arab countries in general, including
Lebanon. Furthermore, the paper attempts to point out the alleged
linkage between Lebanese and Palestinian factors which govern the impact
of the Palestinian armed presence on Lebanese politics, together with
other relevant factors external to the Lebanese environment.

1. The Palestinian armed resistance and the Arab countries after 1967

It is beyond the scope of this paper to discuss in detail Palestinian-Arab
relations in general or the bilateral relationships between the Palestinian
resistance movement and the individual Arab countries in particular.

Rather, the paper provides a brief view of the features which character-ized the Palestinian resistance and its relations with the host Arab coun-tries during the post–June 1967 period.

On the Palestinian level, the re-emergence of the Palestinian armed resistance and its rapid development re-introduced the Palestinians as one of the main parties in the Arab-Israeli conflict and restored the Pales-tinian dimension to this conflict.   The defeat of Arab conventional forces in the June war of 1967 constituted the immediate background for the wide-spread popular Arab support for the Palestinian resistance as an alter-native source of Arab power.   This support, along with the consequently decreasing abilities of the regimes of some Arab host countries to support or control the emergence of the resistance, especially during 1968-69, lead to the expansion of the resistance movement and to its attaining a relatively greater freedom of action within Arab host countries as com-pared with the pre–June 1967 period.   In contrast to the pre-1948 period, however, the Palestinian resistance movement had to establish an extra-territorial presence so far as the Palestinian territory was concerned as a result of the Israeli occupation of all Palestinian territories during June 1967, and of the Israeli tightening of repressive measures against Pales-tinian attempts to develop internal resistance.   The period from 1948 up to June 1967 did not witness the establishment of an effective Palestinian resistance movement, whether in the West Bank or in the territories of Arab countries adjacent to Israel on account of the control exercised by these Arab countries on Palestinian military and political activity.

On the level of Palestinian-Arab relations, the post–June 1967 period has seen a closer interaction between inter-Arab and Palestinian politics and a stronger interrelationship between the Palestinian and Arab dimen-sions of the Arab-Israeli conflict.   On the Arab side, the heightened involvement of the Arab host countries in the Arab-Israeli conflict is attributable to three main factors: 1) the Israeli occupation of part of the territories of some of these countries (Syria and Egypt);   2) the establishment of Palestinian guerrilla bases on, and the conducting of guerrilla operations across, the territories of some of these countries (Jordan, Lebanon and Syria);   3) the attempts by some of these Arab host countries to make the Palestinian question an issue in the inter-Arab disputes and rivalries.   On the Palestinian side, on the other hand, the closer interaction with the Arab countries, especially Egypt, Syria, Jordan, Iraq and Lebanon, could be explained by several factors: 1) the Palestinian military presence, along with the presence of Palestinian refugees in some of these Arab countries;   2) the increasing Palestinian dependence on popular and official Arab support in the

military, political and economic fields: 3)   the presence in the Palestinian resistance movement of some organisations which were created and/
or supported by some Arab countries: Al-Sa'iqa by Syria, the   Arab
Liberation Front of Iraq, the Action Organisation for the Liberation of
Palestine and the Palestine Arab Organisation by Egypt.

The intensified Palestinian-Arab interaction during the post-June 1967
period has been accompanied by fluctuations in the relationships between
the resistance movement and the Arab confrontation states (Egypt, Syria,
Iraq, Jordan and Lebanon).   These relationships ranged from rapprochement to friction, depending on: 1) the stances advocated by the ruling
regimes towards the political settlement of the Arab-Israeli conflict;
2) the attempts made by some Arab regimes to pull the resistance into
the inter-Arab political disputes, as well as those made by some resistance organisations to seek the support of some Arab regimes against
those others whose stances on the political settlement diverged from
theirs;   and 3) the lack of readiness by Arab regimes to tolerate the impact of the Palestinian military presence in their countries on their
domestic politics as well as on their defence policies against Israeli
retaliatory action.   The friction between the Palestinian resistance and
some Arab confrontation states resulted from the interactions between two
factors: the divergence between Palestinian and some Arab attitudes
towards the political settlement, and the implications of the Palestinian
guerrilla actions.   The friction was more acute between the resistance
movement and Jordan and Lebanon due to the Palestinian military activities from and across their territories.   Syria, on the other hand,
exercised a more strict control of the Palestinian military presence on
her territory.   The perceived divergence between the political objectives
and strategies of the Palestinians and those of some of the Arab confrontation states, so far as the Arab-Israeli conflict is concerned, was potent-
ially existent during the pre-June 1967 period but was hidden by the
absence of an effective Palestinian military resistance movement.   The
re-emergence of the Palestinian armed resistance after 1967, however,
pushed this Palestinian-Arab friction onto the surface and made it more
acute as a result of the impact generated by the resistance on the politics
of Arab confrontation states and the reciprocal impact of the attempts
made by some of these states to influence, control and/or manipulate the
resistance movement.

From the Arab point of view, one can trace the impact of the Palestinian armed resistance on Arab politics on two levels:
1   On the level of the Arab-Israeli conflict, the resistance movement is
perceived as a factor of political and military instability.   Militarily,

the Palestinian guerrilla action acts as a trigger to Arab-Israeli armed action by inciting Israeli reprisal action. Politically, the Palestinian armed resistance movement hinders the achievement of a permanent political settlement of the Arab-Israeli conflict, to the extent that it can inhibit the attempts by some Arab states to push for such a settlement. In comparison with other Arab confrontation states, Jordan and then Lebanon witnessed a higher degree of military instability across their borders with Israel, due to the Palestinian military activities across their territories.

2   On the level of the Arab domestic environment the impact of the resistance has been conditioned by the peculiarities and uniqueness of each Arab domestic setting as well as by the ideological orientations underlying the Arab policies of the Palestinian resistance organisations. The Palestinian attitudes toward the domestic politics of the host Arab countries ranged from Al-Fatah's declared principle of 'non-interference in the internal affairs of Arab states' to the PFLP's (Popular Front for the Liberation of Palestine) and PDFLP's (Popular Democratic Front for the Liberation of Palestine) declared objectives of antagonising the 'reactionary' Arab regimes. The cross-cutting interaction between these two Palestinian stances and the domestic settings of the Arab host countries rendered the impact of the resistance on the politics of each of these countries rather unique. For example, the Palestinian military presence in Syria did not precipitate a Syrian-Palestinian crisis and armed confrontation as has happened in both Jordan and Lebanon. Moreover, the nature and dynamics of the Palestinian involvement in the Palestinian-Jordanian crisis of 1970 and in the present Lebanese civil war are different, irrespective of the common characteristics manifested in both cases. From another angle, the Palestinian military presence in both Jordan and Lebanon was perceived to have posed a challenge to the local authorities in the light of the local as well as the Arab support it gained. It could also be maintained, from a leftist perspective, that the Palestinian resistance movement is considered a revolutionising element in Arab politics in general, and in the domestic environments of some Arab host countries (Jordan and Lebanon) in particular. The resistance has been playing this revolutionising role through raising the political consciousness of Arab masses, as well as through strengthening anti-status quo and radical forces. To the extent that the status quo forces in the Arab domestic environments rejected this revolutionising role of the resistance and attempted to suppress it, there arose varying degrees of local tension. By playing this role, the resistance can be considered as a factor of domestic instability to the extent that the local authorities could not

exercise control over the resistance organisations and to the extent that the resistance contributed to the proliferation of arms among the local anti-status quo forces, thus militarising the local environment.   This analysis would apply more to Jordan and Lebanon than to Syria and Egypt due to the latter's control of Palestinian military activities within and across their territories.

The Arab impact on the Palestinian resistance, on the other hand, could be examined from two angles.   In the first place, by sponsoring the creation of Palestinian resistance organisations, some Arab states have contributed to the multiplicity and proliferation of Palestinian resistance groups.   To the extent that the above Palestinian organisations have given priority to their affiliation with the sponsoring Arab regimes, the Palestinian central authorities (whether the PLO or the Central Committee of the Palestinian resistance) could not exercise control over the behaviour of these organisations within the host Arab countries.   This lack of strict control by the central Palestinian authorities over the actions of the different resistance organisations played an important role in the deterioration of relationships between the resistance movement and the local authorities, as in the cases of Jordan and Lebanon.

In the second place, some Arab countries (Iraq, Libya, Syria and Egypt) have channelled inter-Arab disputes into the resistance movement through the resistance organisations created and/or supported by these countries.   This Arab impact, coupled with the problem of the diversity of Palestinian resistance groups from which the resistance movement has been already suffering, magnified and complicated the impact of the Palestinian armed resistance on the politics of some Arab host countries, especially Lebanon.

II.   The development of the Palestinian armed presence in the Lebanon since 1967: an overview.

The Palestinian presence in the Lebanon dates back to 1948 when an estimated number of 141,882 refugees, mainly from North Palestine (Eastern and Western Galilee) moved into Lebanon after the war.   At present, however, the number of Palestinians refugees in Lebanon amounts to about 275-300,000, mainly distributed among seventeen refugee camps. While the pre-June 1967 period witnessed occasional Palestinian attempts to infiltrate the occupied territories through the Lebanese-Israeli borders, it was only a few months after the June war of 1967 that the Palestinians had started to establish an armed presence in the Lebanon. From that time up to the present, the Palestinian armed presence in the Lebanon could be said to have passed through the following phases, so far as its development is concerned:

1   First phase: From October 1968 - November 1969

On the Palestinian side, the commando build-up began in October 1968, starting with infiltrations into South Lebanon and then spreading later into the Palestinian refugee camps.   Palestinian commandos were trying to establish guerrilla bases and at the same time conducting military operations across the Lebanese-Israeli borders.   It was estimated that during the second half of October 1968 an average of ten incidents per day, including military operations and full-scale battles with regular Israeli troops, took place across Lebanese-Israeli borders.   On the Lebanese side, however, the initial reaction during this phase was two-fold: Moslem and leftist groups and parties supported the Palestinian military presence in Lebanon, while the local authorities attempted to exercise tighter control over Palestinian military activities within and across the country. In this connection the Israelis exerted pressure on the Lebanese authorities to push them into taking restrictive measures against the Palestinian military activities by conducting retaliatory actions.   These came to a climax on 28 December 1968, with an Israeli raid on Beirut airport which lasted 45 minutes and destroyed thirteen airliners.   That Israeli raid later precipitated a Lebanese Cabinet crisis when Prime Minister Abdullah Yafi resigned on 8 January 1969, after a criticism of his government's handling of the raid.   The Israeli reprisal action escalated tension by inciting guerrilla counter-military action across the Lebanese territory and precipitating Palestinian clashes with the Lebanese army and security forces.   A serious series of clashes broke out on 23 April 1969, when Lebanese security forces attempted to break up a Palestinian demonstration coming out from Ain-El-Helweh refugee camp to Sidon, a city in South Lebanon.   Clashes spread into other Lebanese cities and a state of emergency was declared.   Prime Minister Rashid Karami tendered his resignation on April 25 and the country stayed without a prime minster for seven months.   The Lebanese President Charles Helou was reported to have called for an end to the Palestinian commando presence in the Lebanon and to have objected to the establishment of commando bases or training grounds there.

A series of more serious clashes between Palestinian guerrillas and the Lebanese army, erupting into a major crisis, occurred in the second half of October 1969.   The clashes started in South Lebanon but spread into other parts of the country and continued until early November.   By 3 November, and as a result of Egyptian mediation efforts, a Lebanese army delegation, headed by the then Commander-in-Chief of the Lebanese army Major-General Emile Bustani, met with a Palestinian delegation headed by Yasir Arafat and signed an agreement which later became known

as the 'Cairo Agreement'. The agreement granted the Palestinian resistance the right of autonomous administrative control of the refugee camps
in the Lebanon, permitted the Palestinians resident in Lebanon to
'participate in the Palestinian revolution through armed struggle' and
provided for the facilitation of commando movement in and their way into
the Arkoub region in South Lebanon. In other words, this agreement
could be considered an explicit legitimization, from the Lebanese official
point of view, of the Palestinian military presence in the Lebanon.
Having embodied an acceptance of the Palestinian military presence in the
Lebanon, the agreement attempted to reconcile the Lebanese sovereignty
with the implications of the Palestinian military presence in the country,
through containing several provisions to regulate the Lebanese relations
with the resistance movement. Such provisions stipulated that the local
Palestinian committees in the camps should cooperate with the Lebanese
authorities; that there should be coordination between the Lebanese
security forces and the Palestinian Armed Struggle Command, so that the
latter would control the actions of Palestinian commandos and ensure
their non-interference in Lebanese affairs; that the entry, exit and movements of Palestinian commandos should be regulated and that the resistance should accept the principle that the Lebanese authorities exercise full
responsibility and authority over all Lebanese territory.

2   The Second Phase: From November 1969 - Spring 1973
On the Lebanese level, the signing of the 'Cairo Agreement' was followed
by Prime Minister Rashid Karami's formation of a new cabinet on 25
November 1969, whereby the new Interior Minister, Kamal Jumblat,
was delegated the responsibility of regulating the Lebanese relations with
the resistance movement. Later on, 4th February 1970, Jumblat was
reported to have reached an agreement with the resistance to the effect
that the commandos would freeze their military operations across the
Lebanese-Israeli borders, that they would stay at distances of at least
one kilometer away from villages in South Lebanon, and that the resistance
would stop conducting military training in the refugee camps.   Two
Palestinian-Lebanese co-ordinating committees were reported to have
been formed and charged with implementing this agreement.
     On the other hand, the 'Cairo Agreement' elicited strong criticism
from the Lebanese Phalange Party to the extent that its leader, Pierre
Gemayel sent a note to the Lebanese prime minister, on 5th June 1969,
condemning the agreement and asserting that it was tantamount to a loss
of Lebanese sovereignty.   In the meantime, the Israelis reacted to the
signing of the 'Cairo Agreement' by intensifying their retaliatory action

against Lebanon and threatening publicly to increase this action if the
Lebanese authorities would not suppress Palestinian military activities
from Lebanese territories.   Two such Israeli public threats were made
respectively by Moshe Dayan, then Israeli Defence Minister, on 10 May
and by Yigal Allon, then Deputy Prime Minister, on 13 May 1970. Later
on the 27th of the same month, the Lebanese cabinet decided to prohibit
the carrying of arms in public, and approved a proposal made by the
Interior Minister to ban the firing of rockets from Lebanese territory.

On the Palestinian side, the early part of this phase, 1970-71, witnessed a reduction in guerrilla action across the Lebanese-Israeli borders
borders, due mainly to the involvement of the resistance movement in the
crisis with the Jordanian authorities in September 1970 and the summer
of 1971, which lead to the suppression of Palestinian military presence
in Jordan.   In view of these developments in Jordan, and the attempts of
Lebanese authorities to impose restrictions on the guerrilla action across
the Lebanese-Israeli borders, the years 1972-73 saw attempts by
Palestinian commandos to conduct military operations from outside Arab
territories.   Two examples on these Palestinian attempts were the
attack on the Lydda Airport on 30 May 1972, sponsored by the PFLP, and
that on the Israeli section of the Olympics in Munich, on 5 September of
the same year.   In both cases, however, the Israeli authorities charged
Lebanon with responsibility for the operations due to the Palestinian
military presence on its territory.   Militarily, the Israelis reacted to
the resistance operations by conducting retaliatory action against South
Lebanon as well as against Palestinian commando targets inside the
country.   The climax of Israeli retaliatory action was to occur later on
9-10 April 1973, in an attack on Beirut in which three Palestinian resistance leaders (Kamal Nasser, Abu Yusuf and Kamal Adwan) were killed.
This attack precipitated a Lebanese cabinet crisis, when Prime Minister
Saab Salam resigned putting the blame on the Commander-in-Chief of the
Lebanese army, General Iskander Ghanem, for the shortcomings of the
army and of the security forces in the action. The Palestinian-Lebanese
tension generated by the Israeli attack exploded later on 2 May of the same
year, into a new series of serious armed clashes between the Lebanese
army and the Palestinian resistance forces.   The clashes continued until
17 May when a new Lebanese-Palestinian agreement was reached and the
state of emergency declared on 8 May, was abolished.   Although it
supported the provisions of the 'Cairo Agreement', the new agreement
was reported by Lebanese military authorities to have included provisions
for prohibiting the bearing of arms or the wearing of battledress by
commandos in the city streets, the co-operation of the resistance with

Lebanese authorities in investigating cases involving Palestinians, and an agreement to settle, in subsequent meetings, the problem of heavy arms in the refugee camps.

3   The Third Phase: Summer 1973 to 13 April 1975

The attempts made by some Lebanese political parties (notably the Phalangists and former President Camille Chamoun's National Liberal party) to establish military training camps for their militias, were subjects of critical discussion in some Lebanese newspapers early in this phase. In reaction to these criticisms, the Phalangist party leader claimed, on 17 September 1973, the right of his party to establish such camps and refused to close them. In addition, Mr Nasri Maaluf, then Lebanese Defence Minister, also justified these attempts as a reaction to the freedom given to the Palestinians in Lebanon, through the 'Cairo Agreement,' to carry arms. By late September this issue precipitated another cabinet crisis when Takiyyudin Sulh, Prime Minister since 21 June 1973, resigned on 25 September. The crisis was triggered by the resignation, on 18 September, of two ministers who were followers of Kamal Jumblat, Bahij Takiyyidin, Interior Minister, and Tawfiq Assaf, Minister of Oil and Industry. Later Jumblat explained the resignations as a reaction to the lack of government action to prohibit the import of arms by the two previously-mentioned Lebanese political parties. On 18 September, the Lebanese cabinet banned the possession of firearms, but this was too late to prevent the resignation of the two ministers.

On the Palestinian side, some resistance sources declared publicly, first on 9 March and then in early July 1974, that the commandos would freeze their military activities from the Lebanese territories, so as not to provoke the Israelis into conduct retaliatory action against Lebanon. However, this declared policy did not inhibit Israeli reprisal actions in the light of the continued Palestinian guerrilla action inside as well as outside the occupied territories. For example, the Israelis attacked villages and two Palestinian refugee camps in South Lebanon, on 16 May 1974, as a reaction to the guerrilla attack on Ma'alot on the previous day. Furthermore, in early January 1975, the Israelis conducted what they called 'preventive' attacks against Lebanese and Palestinian targets in South Lebanon. On 20 January, Lebanon called for a meeting of the Arab Defence Cluncil to discuss such Israeli aggression. On the other hand, the Phalange party leader sent a notice to the Lebanese President Franjieh on 24 January, criticizing Lebanon's attitude of compromise towards the Palestinian military presence. Later on 20 February, Gemayal called for a referendum on the relations between the Lebanese

government and the Palestinian resistance movement and claimed that at
least sixty percent of the Lebanese population would share his party's
view that the government was not exercising enough authority over the
resistance and was losing its control over South Lebanon.

This mounting internal tension was later intensified as a result of the
clashes between the Lebanese army and demonstrators in Sidon protest-
ing, on 26 February, against the government's granting of a licence to a
fishing enterprise (The Protein Company) which they maintained would
affect the livelihood of the local fishermen.   These clashes, in which
Saida's former deputy, Ma'aruf Sa'ad was wounded and later died, provoked tension and demonstrations in other Lebanese cities.   This tension
constituted the immediate background for the incident, which occurred
at Air-Rummanah, in Beirut on 13 April 1975, and which triggered the
present Lebanese civil war.   This was an attack by some Phalangist
militia men on a bus carrying Palestinians - as well as other Lebanese,
on their way back from the Shatila to the Tal-Za'atar refugee camp in
Beirut, where they had been attending a rally to mark the first anniver-
saryof the Palestinian guerrilla attack on the Israeli settlement of
Qiryat Shmona.   The incident opened a new phase in the development of
the Palestinian military presence in the Lebanon, which will be the
subject of discussion in the following section.

III   The Palestinian resistance movement and the present civil war in
the Lebanon

Preliminary to a discussion of the Palestinian involvement in the present
Lebanese civil war, two general remarks should be made:

1   The war is characterized by a multiplicity of parties and issues.
For an adequate understanding of the factors at issue and a clear
identification of the parties involved, one should pay attention to
four levels of analysis: the Lebanese, the Palestinian, the Arab
and the international levels.   The dynamics of the present civil
have to a large extent been governed by the interaction of factors
from all four levels.

2   Apart from the Arab and international factors involved in the war
and apart from the Palestinian armed presence, there are four
Lebanese dimensions: Sectarian (Christian against Moslem
groups), socio-economic (unprivileged against privileged classes),
political (pan-Arabists against Lebanese nationalists), and the
struggle for power and influence among the local Lebanese leadership.   However, it is the interaction between these four dimensions
which makes it difficult to establish priorities among the roles

played by each.   A clear example of the inter-relationship of these four
dimensions is provided by the composition of the Nasserite groups which
are fighting on the Moslem and leftist sides: The members of these
groups are predominantly Moslem, pan-Arab oriented, coming mostly
from unprivileged classes, and their leadership is struggling for more
power and influence in the local politics of the country.   Thus, any
explanation that singles out just one of the four Lebanese dimensions as
characrerizing the present civil war, to the exclusion of the others,   is
misleading.

It is one of the theses of this paper that the Palestinian resistance
movement was dragged into the crisis, which escalated into the present
civil war in Lebanon, through an interplay of Palestinian, Lebanese as
well as other Arab and international factors.

On the Lebanese level, the main motive of the Phalange and, later,
the National Liberal parties, which were tacitly supported by the Lebanese
president Suleiman Franjieh, was to precipitate a Lebanese-Palestinian
crisis leading to the suppression of the Palestinian military presence in
the Lebanon, and thus to the weakening of the position of Moslem and
leftist groups which were demanding a change in the Lebanese political
system.   The Phalangist strategy was to keep the conflict strictly as one
of Lebanese versus Palestinian, and thus to create conditions for the
intervention of the Lebanese army to tip the military balance against the
Palestinian resistance.   The Phalangists succeeded in pulling the Palestinian resistance into the crises but failed to suppress the Lebanese
dimension of the conflict, while the Lebanese army intervened only in a
limited degree and later was subject to splits which rendered its role
in the crisis ineffective.   On the other hand, support for the Palestinian
resistance by Lebanese Moslem and leftist groups reinforced the latter's
demand for a change in Lebanese political system and, perhaps,
encouraged them to intensify the crisis.

On the Palestinian level, the attitude of the resistance organisations
was two-fold.   It has been maintained, on the one hand, that the
Palestinian 'Rejection Front' (comprising the Popular Front for the
Liberation, the Arab Liberation Front, the Popular Front for the Liberation of Palestine-General Command, and the Popular Struggle Front)
promoted the crisis as a reaction to the attempts being made, and allegedly
supported by the PLO, to settle the Arab-Israeli conflict politically.   On
the other hand, Al-Fateh, along with other Palestinian organisations,
attempted to keep the resistance movement from being dragged into the
crisis in order to secure the position of the Palestinian military presence in Lebanon, in view of the suppression of the Palestinian resistance

in Jordan and the control exercised by Syria on Palestinian military
activities.

On the external level, it has been maintained that Israel and the United
States and in varying degrees Egypt and Jordan, were interested in seeing
the Palestinian military action being suppressed or in the least controlled,
so that the resistance would not be able to hinder the achievement of a
political settlement through triggering Arab-Israeli armed action.   On
the other hand, Libya and Iraq supported the stand and reaction of the
Palestinian 'Rejection Front' towards the political settlement attempts.
Syria was interested in inhibiting the Lebanese crisis and stabilizing the
situation there because it had foreseen prospects for reaching another
territorial agreement with Israel over the Golan Heights.

The degree and form of the Palestinian involvement in the civil war
were determined by the continued interaction among the above-mentioned
policies and the internal and external variables affecting the development
of the war.   Up to the present, the Palestinian involvement in the war
could be said to have passed through four stages

The first stage extended from 13 April 1975, when the incident at Ain-
Rummanah took place, to the formation of Lebanese military cabinet on
23 May, under the premiership of Brigadier Nur-eddin Rifai.   During
this stage, the conflict was primarily between the Phalange party and the
Palestinian resistance.   This was due to the fact that most of the people
killed during the attack at the bus at Ain-Rummanah were Palestinians,
several of whom belonged to the Arab Liberation Front.   During this
stage, one should distinguish between the degree and form of involvement
by members of Palestinian 'Rejection Front' and those of other Palestinian resistance organisations.   Al-Fateh and As-Saiqa, along with other
Palestinian organisations, were politically involved, trying to pressure
the Lebanese authorities to arrest the Phalangist elements responsible
for the Ain-Rummanah incident.   The involvement of the 'Rejection Front'
elements was relatively more military in nature, and took the form of
limited clashes with some Phalangist elements.   However, as the Lebanese
Prime Minister, Rashid Sulh, resigned on 16 May, and a military cabinet
was formed on 23 May, the Lebanese dimension to the conflict was pushed
to the surface and became predominant.

The second stage began with the rejection of the military cabinet by
Lebanese Moslem leadership communicated to President Franjieh
by Kamal Jumblat on 24 May.   As a result, Brigadier Rifai sub-
mitted the resignation of his cabinet on 25 May and Rashid Karami was
entrusted, on 28th May, with the formation of a new cabinet. The formation of the new cabinet, on 30 June, was preceded by a three-hour meeting

between Yasir Afafat and President Franjieh, in which it was agreed to
enforce the 'Cairo Agreement' of 1969 as well as that of May 1973. Moreover, Arafat also agreed to give a statement of policy on the part of the
PLO concerning Palestinian-Lebanese relations. This statement, which
was broadcast on Lebanese radio and television on 25 June, maintained
that the Palestinians would unconditionally support Lebanese sovereignty,
that they would not get involved in Lebanese affairs, that they would not
support any Lebanese faction against the other, and that they acknowledged
that the resistance movement depended on the security and stability of
Lebanon. The PLO leadership attempted to make a balance between
sticking to the above-declared Palestinian policy and giving limited support
to the Moslem and leftist groups in order to guarantee, in return, the
latter's support to the Palestinian military presence in Lebanon. This
ambivalent attitude resulted in a limited military involvement by Al-Fateh
and As-Saiqa which took the form of giving some arms to some Moslems
and leftist groups, defending some Moslem areas against Phalangist
attacks and supporting Moslem and leftist attacks against some Phalangist
targets. Politically, however, the PLO leadership acted at times in the
role of a mediator, by co-operating with the Lebanese authorities in order
to arrange for cease-fires and by agreeing to police these ceasefires in
co-ordination with Lebanese security forces. On the other hand, the
'Rejection Front' organisations got comparatively more involved militarily
during this stage, justifying their fighting on the side of Moslem and
leftist groups, partly on ideological grounds, and partly to hinder attempts
to settle the Arab-Israeli conflict politically. These stances, advocated
respectively by the PLO leadership and the 'Rejection Front', continued
more or less to characterize the Palestinian involvement in the civil war
during this stage, until 4 January 1976 when Phalangist and other Christian
militia forces blocked Tal-Za'atar and Jisr al-Basha refugee camps in
Beirut.

The blockade of the two Palestinian camps opened a third stage in the
Palestinian involvement by pulling the resistance into the fighting on a
larger scale, thus restoring the Palestinian dimension to the civil war.
On the Palestinian level this development reduced the polarization between
the PLO's and 'Rejection Front's' stances in the war by pushing them
both in the direction of more military involvement. The fighting escalated
rapidly when Phalangist forces besieged the Palestinian refugee camp of
Dhbai, north of Beirut, and occupied it on 13 January. On the same day,
the Lebanese Maronite leadership held a summit meeting in Ba'abda,
after which they issued a statement, which maintained that the present
conflict in Lebanon was a Palestinian-Lebanese one. In retaliation to the

Phalangist blockade of the camps, Moslem and leftist forces, aided by
Palestinian resistance, blockaded the Christian town of Damour and the
village of Al-Jiyya, south of Beirut.   At this stage, and by the time the
Phalangist forces committed what was later called the 'Qarantina massacre"
in Beirut on 18 January, the Lebanese and the Palestinian dimensions of
the war became more intertwined through the heightened involvement of the
resistance forces in the fighting.   Later, and through Syrian mediation,
an agreement was reached on 14 February, to have a ceasefire, after which
President Franjieh announced a new Lebanese 'Constitutional Declaration',
which will be discussed in the last section of this paper.   Along with this
Declaration, however, an agreement was reached to adhere to the previous
Palestinian-Lebanese agreements of 1969 and 1973 concerning the Palestinian military presence in Lebanon.   However, in view of the continuation
of the conflict in spite of the announcement of the above 'Declaration',
Brigadier Aziz Ahdab attempted to make a coup d'etat on 1 March 1976,
and demanded the resignation of both the President and the Prime Minister.
The persistent refusal of President Franjieh to resign triggered a new
stage in the escalation of fighting in the country.

During the early phase of the new, fourth, stage, the resistance played
a two-sided role.   On the one hand, the PLO leadership attempted to ease
the rising tension between Syria, which was trying to stabilise the conflict
situation, and Moslem and leftist groups, which were escalating the fighting in an attempt to force the resignation of President Franjieh.   On the
other hand, the resistance forces, mainly from the 'Rejection Front',
were participating in the fighting on the side of the Moslem and leftist
groups.   Later, during this stage, and in view of the actual Syrian intervention and of Palestinian anticipation of Syrian attempts to reach another
settlement over the Golan Heights, there occurred a shift in alliances
among the Palestinian resistance organisations.   In parts of the country
some Palestinian forces in the Syrian-controlled As-Saiqa and the Palestine
Liberation Army acted as a buffer, to separate the fighting forces on
either side.   There were also instances in which some Palestinian elements
from these organisations were reported to have participated in the fighting on the side of the Christian forces.

Due to the rapid development of the civil war in Lebanon, it would be
risky to speculate about the changes that might occur in the Palestinian
involvement in this war, in the immediate future.   However, it is
expected that Arab factors (especially Syrian) will play a rather important
role in influencing the degree and form of the Palestinian movement.

The Palestinian involvement is also conditioned by the attempts of some Lebanese factions to pull the resistance movement into the fighting, as well as by the consequent reactions of the Palestinian resistance organisations.

IV   The impact of the Palestinian armed presence on Lebanese politics: an appraisal

The impact of the Palestinian armed presence on Lebanese politics could be examined on three levels   the Arab-Israeli conflict, the Lebanese relations with the Arab world, and the Lebanese domestic environment.

The Palestinian armed presence has heightened Lebanon's political as well as military involvement in the Arab-Israeli conflict. Militarily, the resistance triggered armed action across the Lebanese-Israeli borders through inciting Israeli retaliatory action. Politically, the Palestinian presence started Lebanon's involvement in the Arab political efforts connected with the search for a settlement to the Palestinian problem. Lebanon shared this inpact of the Palestinian armed presence with Jordan and it would have shared it with Syria if the latter did not exercise control on the Palestinian military activities from its territories. However, one would qualify the above statement by saying that Lebanon became more vulnerable to this impact after the suppression of the Palestinian resistance in Jordan in 1970-71. Moreover, the Israeli retaliatory action exerted pressure on the Lebanese domestic environment through forcing a number of Lebanese to move from the South into Beirut and other areas in Lebanon. It has been estimated that by July 1969, the number of Lebanese who moved from the South amounted to 22,853.

On another level, it is maintained that the Palestinian armed presence has contributed to what is called the 'Arabisation' of Lebanese politics. Besides heightening the Lebanese involvement in the Arab-Israeli conflict, this Arabisation has two other aspects. On the one hand, the resistance movement has acted as a carrier of Arab influence and inter-Arab disputes into the Lebanese setting. The resistance has played this role reluctantly as a result of the attempts of some Arab countries to extend their influence into the movement by creating and/or supporting some resistance organisations. On the other hand, the resistance movement has contributed to the Pan-Arab consciousness of some sectors of the Lebanese community, especially on the Moslem and leftist sides. These groups, in turn, supported the demand for more involvement on the part of Lebanon in Arab affairs, especially those connected with the Arab-Israeli conflict.

On the level of Lebanese domestic setting, the Palestinian resistance

acted as a factor of change and instability.   The resistance is perceived
by the Phalangists and other Maronite groups as a force pushing Lebanon
away from the Lebanese 'National Pact' of 1943.   For besides 'Arabising'
the Lebanese politics, the resistance is considered to have strengthened
the position of the Moslem and leftist forces which are attempting to disturb
the sectarian balance established through the above 'Pact'.   One could
cite some of the items embodied in the 'Constitutional Declaration' announced by President Franjieh on 14 February 1976, as partial evidence
for the plausibility of this argument: the new 'Constitutional Declaration'
granted more powers to the Lebanese Prime Minister, a post controlled
by the Moslem Sunnites, and provided for an equal distribution of seats
in the parliamentary committees between Moslems and Christians - in
contrast to the 5:6 proportion provided by the 'Pact' of 1943.   However,
it would be invalid to argue that the presence of the Palestinians, who
are predominantly Moslem, has increased the Lebanese Moslem majority,
and thus tipped the sectarian balance, in view of the fact that the Palestinians have not been granted the rights of Lebanese citizenship and hence
do not have the power to affect Lebanese political elections.

The change in the Lebanese political system resulting from the presence
of the Palestinian resistance was to occur gradually through the de-
stabilization of the Lebanese domestic setting.   From this perspective ,
the resistance is considered to have acted as a catalyst in introducing
domestic instability.   For, in addition to strengthening the position of
the Moslem and leftist anti-status quo forces politically, the resistance
also contributed to the militarisation of the Lebanese political environment.
Besides training, recruiting and/or providing some arms to the above two
Lebanese groups, the Palestinian military presence provided an excuse
for these groups, along with the Phalange and other Christian groups, to
import arms from different sources.   Hence, further instability was
generated as a result of availability of new military options to the already
conflicting Lebanese factions.

In conclusion, it should be maintained that so long as the Palestinian
military presence in Lebanon continues to exist, and so long as no settlement to the Arab-Israeli conflict acceptable to the Palestinians is reached,
Lebanon will still suffer from the impact of the Palestinian military
presence on its territory.

Sources

Al-Kitab As-Sanawi Lil-Qadhiyya Al-Filastinia 1969 and 1970 ('The Palestine Year-book) (Beirut The Institute for Palestine Studies)

Al-Wathaig Al-Filastinia Al-Arabiyya, 1969 ('Palestinian Arab Documents ments') (Beirut: The Institute for Palestine Studies)

Arab Report and Record, 1967-76

El-Rayyes, Riad and Nahas, Duria, eds Guerrillas For Palestine, A Study of the Palestinian Commando Organizations (Beirut, An-Nahar Press Services, 1974)

Harkabi, Y 'Fedayeen Action and Arab Strategy', Adelphi Papers 53 (London: The International Institute for Strategic Studies 1968).

Hurewitz, J C ed Soviet-American Rivalry in the Middle East (New York, 1969)

Laffin, John Fedayeen, the Arab Dilemma (London, 1973)

Nadwat Ad-Dirasat Al-Inmaiyya, Lubnan Wal-A'mal Al-Fidai Al-Filestinii ('Lebanon and the Palestinian Commando Action') (Beirut, 1969)

O'Ballance, Edgar Arab Guerrilla Power, 1967-72 (London, 1974)

El-Rayyes,Riad and Nahas, Dunia eds Guerrillas For Palestine, A Study of the Palestinian Commando Organizations (Beirut: An-Nahar Press Services, 1974)

Schmidt, Dana, Adams Armageddon in the Middle East (New York,1974)

MERIP Report, 44 (1975)

Sharabi, Hisham, Palestine Guerrillas: Their Credibility and Effectiveness (Washington, DC, 1970)

As-Siyasa Ad-Dawliyya ('International Affairs'), (January 1976)

Journal of the Palestine Studies, 3 (Spring, 1972) and IV,2 (Winter,1975)

Shoun Filestiniyya ('Palestine Affairs'), 50-51 (October, 1975)

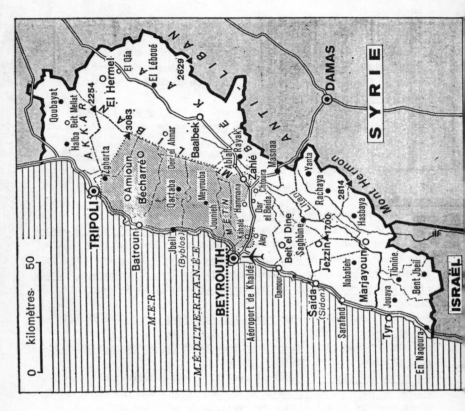

☐ Zones contrôlées par les forces islamo-progressistes et palestiniennes

▨ Réduit chrétien conservateur

Note that the Kura district surrounds Amioun

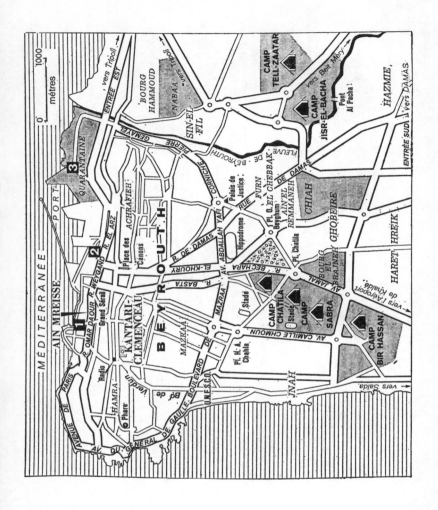

Maps reprinted from <u>Le Monde</u>